JESUS
LOVES ME

JESUS
LOVES ME

*Celebrating the Profound Truths
of a Simple Hymn*

CALVIN MILLER

WARNER BOOKS

An AOL Time Warner Company

Warner Books, Inc., 1271 Avenue of the Americas, New York, NY 10020

Visit our Web site at www.twbookmark.com.

 An AOL Time Warner Company

Printed in the United States of America

First Printing: April 2002

10 9 8 7 6 5 4 3 2 1

Library of Congress Cataloging-in-Publication Data

Miller, Calvin.
    Jesus loves me : celebrating the profound truths of a simple hymn / Calvin Miller.
       p. cm.
      ISBN 0-446-52920-6
       1. Jesus Christ—Person and offices. 2. Warner, Anna Bartlett, 1824–1915. Jesus loves me. I. Title

BT203.M54 2001
264'.23—dc21

2001055942

Book design and text composition by L&G McRee

To Barbara

JESUS LOVES ME

Jesus loves me! This I know,
For the Bible tells me so;
Little ones to Him belong;
They are weak, but He is strong.

Jesus loves me! He who died
Heaven's gate to open wide!
He will wash away my sin,
Let His little child come in

Jesus loves me! He will stay
Close beside me all the way,
If I love Him when I die
He will take me home on high.

ANNA B. WARNER, 1860

CONTENTS

JESUS
LOVES ME

Christianity is immense, but Jesus is even bigger. Jesus is the hero of Western civilization.

Year after year Jesus appears on the front of *Time, Newsweek,* and myriad other magazines and tabloids. He is the ever-circling subject of talk shows, television specials, and national passion plays. He is the ageless center of Western culture—all-encompassing in his influence. He is the dividing line laid down through the middle of human history. The time designations B.C.E. and C.E. contain the root of his name to mark the center of the rising and falling centuries.

But it is not the Christ for all time that most appeals to me. It is the Christ of my time. For this great Christ has now come to me, declaring his love. He has gilded my dismal unimportance with meaning. In the cosmic clockwork, he has touched my micron status and made it large. I am loved. Jesus has replaced my meaninglessness with significance. Jesus spent heaven and purchased me. What a price he paid! How valuable I am, and yet I never would have known it except that I collided with God's love.

No wonder the world seems eager to worship at his feet. But culture cannot express the fullness of all that Jesus is. Only Christians can do this. And how do we who call ourselves Christians do it? By offering him our praise—sometimes in exalted ways, sometimes in simpler modes. Even after we hear some great cathedral choir praise him with Handel's *Messiah,* we still desire to adore him with the words of the child's hymn "Jesus Loves Me."

"Jesus Loves Me" is our simple, world-class anthem. It is rooted in our childhood.

Who can chart the varied ways he comes to us? He sometimes comes upon us suddenly in a rush of overwhelming love. His presence is as warm as a desert wind let loose in the Arctic winter of our despair. He sometimes comes more quietly to touch our lives and set God's grandeur dancing with our need. But always his coming brings joy. I have felt it and wept. Why? Because, in the midst of a pointless universe I drink of true significance. I feel Jesus' love. No—I more than feel it. I claim it, deposit it at the bank, and draw daily on the account.

"Jesus loves me" is the heart of all I cherish. Indeed, from year to year I revel in it. Its warmth lingers about me in every instance of threat or pressure. This simple song calms me, strips off my threats, and drains my stress into reservoirs of God's serenity.

The simple hymn at the focus of this book first came to me as a legacy of my mother's love. When I was a child she loved to show me off. She would have me stand and sing "Jesus Loves Me," often to complete strangers, when I was only three. They applauded. My suspicion is that her mother had her singing it to complete strangers when she was only three in 1903, as I had my children singing it to complete strangers when they were only three in 1963. My daughter had my grandson singing it to complete strangers in 1993. Over a century, four generations of Millers have now built upon the musical certainty of this song. It is woven into the fabric of our heritage. The way each new generation of Millers proved we were Christian families was to have our children perform "Jesus Loves Me." We were forced to perform it for our pastor or at the family reunion or to complete strangers. Others were forced to undergo our showbiz testimony merely because they had the ill luck to happen into our home when Mother was feeling full of faith and ultra-musical.

But is there anything really wrong with such musical certainty? Given our chances for cancer, car wrecks, Alzheimer's, and apathy, does it hurt to be a bit exhibitionist about faith? What's wrong with spreading this tune like a titanium shield over the softer ills of our lives?

Diaper rash? Yes, but Jesus loves me.

Job loss? Yes, but Jesus loves me.

Divorce, disgrace, dyspepsia? Yes, yes, yes.

There is much in life to fear: war, disease, loneliness. We cower before simple daytime fears and we are terrified of things that go *bump* in the night. Secular philosophies attack our cherished beliefs. A dour mood creeps into movies, novels, and newscasts. The universe often seems senseless and meaningless. "Eat and defecate, the dish and the pot are the two extremities of man," said playwright Samuel Beckett. Such hopelessness needs the help of a simple child's hymn.

I need this child's hymn.

Jesus is the exclamation point in the prosaic paragraphs of my life. Boredom and weariness are everywhere. But take heart: the dull tale of our pointlessness has met the happy gleam of God's love in Christ!

So in this book I want to call us all to sit and listen to a child's hymn. Our wounds and illnesses have met a simple healing. "Jesus Loves Me" is not a saccharine phrase to embroider in pink needlepoint. These three words are no Pollyanna philosophy. They are as reasonable as Socrates' "Know thyself." They are more dependable than Thomas Edison's cliché, "Genius is 10 percent inspiration and 90 percent perspiration." They offer more hope for our careers than J. P. Getty's capitalist prescription for success, "Get up early, work hard, find oil." They make more eternal sense than Woody Allen's "Eighty percent of success is just showing up." We must set alongside all such proverbs the security of the world's best truth: *Jesus loves me!*

When we see Jesus alive in the most admirable of his saints, such as Mother Teresa, it is hard to walk away from our intrigue with him. We must pursue him, even when our pursuit seems anguished. We reach and he eludes us. Yet we must reach again. Why? Because "Jesus loves me," well lived out, dogs us to pursue him till we at last lay hold of him and then hold on to him till we've praised him.

No wonder Earl Palmer confesses, "If I dismiss him as an idea, he haunts me as a man. If I dismiss him as a man, he haunts me as an idea."[1] When we're inclined to say he never lived, we are still forced to confess, "A life this noble must be real." When we try to dodge his life saying, "He lived, but cannot have done all the things the Bible says he did," then our confession erupts: "Still he is the most noble of all noble ideas."

"Jesus loves me" is a heart cry!

Yet the song may be most valuable when it is least audible. It's only when we've grown older that its melody sometimes seems naïve—too juvenile to confess out loud. Nevertheless, its compelling music lingers. When the compacted subway tubes belch their "eight-to-fivers" out onto the crowded sidewalks of Manhattan, the song survives. There, where the executives of Wall Street read the traveling light strands of the stock market report, the telltale tune lives on.

Tune your ears to listen to anyone whose life isn't working out. Often you will hear this subtle tune of hope. Listen! There it is! It is floating on the frightened air. The song lives—barely audible over our weeping days. An urban requiem of the tired and rich and needy! The entire nation is singing deep down on the inside where life hurts first and heals last:

Jesus loves me! This I know,
For the Bible tells me so;
Little ones to Him belong;
They are weak, but He is strong.

QUESTIONS FOR REFLECTION

1. Can you remember when you first learned "Jesus Loves Me"? If not, can you think of a time when the song had some rather special impact on you?
2. Can you think of a time when, in the midst of crisis, you really felt that Jesus loved you and that just remembering this helped you deal with the problem at hand?
3. What do you think the phrase "If I dismiss him as an idea, he haunts me as a man. If I dismiss him as a man, he haunts me as an idea" really means? What does it mean to you?

CHAPTER 1

Jesus Loves Me: I Can Make It

There is a man whose tomb is guarded by love,
there is a man who sepulchre is not only glorious
as the prophets declared,
but whose sepulchre is loved . . .
There is a man whose every word still vibrates and
produces more than love,
produces virtues fructifying in love.
There is a man, who eighteen centuries ago, was
nailed to gibbet, and whom millions of adorers daily
detach from this throne of his suffering, and
kneeling before him as low as they can without
shame, there upon the earth they kiss his feet with
unspeakable ardor.
There is a man who was scourged, killed, crucified, whom an ineffable passion raises from death
and infamy, and exults to the glory of love unfailing
which finds in Him, peace, honor, joy, and even
ecstasy . . .
There is a man, in fine, and only one, who has
founded his love upon the earth, and that Man is
thyself, O Jesus! who was pleased to baptize me, to
anoint me, to consecrate me in thy love, and whose
name now opens my very heart, and draws from it
those accents which overpower me and raise me
above myself.

JEAN-BAPTISTE-HENRI LACORDAIRE[1]

A CONVERSATION WITH JESUS

Jesus, how can I know you love me?

Let me show you, my child. Consider the lilies of the field; they toil not, neither do they spin. Yet I say unto you that even Solomon in all his glory was not arrayed like one of these. Be sure of this: The God who loves the lilies loves you even more.

But what happens when the breezes stop and the gales begin? Then lilies argue too softly to be heard. When the storms spend their force on my despair, show me no flowers to prove God's love. When the hard times come, grace must come as granite. Peace must be a pier of steel.

You can handle the hard times, for I did. Look to the horizon. See the cross where I died. If you would know the strength of love, watch me bleed. Greater love hath no man than this—that a man lay down his life for his friends.

The cross convinces me you loved the world in general. But what about me? I don't mean to be selfish, Jesus, but there are six billion people on the planet. I would like to know if I have any special meaning to you?

I never loved or died for the masses. I spoke to them but I've never loved any multitude at once. I never will. I cannot love that way. I love only singularly—one person at a time. And you may be sure I have loved you with an everlasting love. The very hairs of your head are numbered. Are not sparrows two a penny, yet not a one of them falls to the earth without my care? Indeed, if you had been the only person who ever needed my love, I still would have loved you.

I am convinced; I've seen the proof. Your bloody wounds tell me how much you love me. Shall I in doubting your love add to your wounds? No, never. All doubt be gone. Jesus loves me, this I know.

MATTHEW 6:28, JOHN 15:13, JEREMIAH 31:3, LUKE 12:6–7

Jesus loves me, this I know.

To be loved and to know it makes every sunrise seem a promise. Whatever lies ahead of us, we are loved. Whatever must be faced, we have a lover. His voice calms the storms. His feet stand firm upon the troubled oceans of our voyage.

Yet we seem like inept anatomy students. Time and again we dissect God's love. Why? We want to know how much we are loved and how long we may expect his love to last. But all love has a built-in shortfall: it never seems enough. So we are driven in our pursuit to have even more of it. At the same time we are the victims of our search, the captives of our longing. It was Augustine who said the whole of the Christian life is longing. Therefore, "Jesus Loves Me" is more than a song from our childhood. It is a heart cry first to know we are loved and second to know how much we are loved.

Still, who of us are not restless waves in search of a shoreline? Why? Who can say? But we are rarely content in life. Our restlessness is kept alive by our restless hearts. Augustine said our hearts remain restless until they find their rest in God. We are evidence of this truth. If ever we gain any ease in life, it comes in the knowledge that somebody, somewhere loves us.

I know this longing firsthand.

I am needy and I can clearly see that a love-neurosis stalks my heart of faith. I am first lost in my searching after love. Then, having found it, I am further lost in analyzing what this love means. But I know I am not alone in this search. God's love haunts all of us till we find it, and then haunts us because we have found it.

All love is both elusive and haunting. Even newly-weds have the odd sensation of waking up the morning after their wedding exulting over their union. Their togetherness seems too rich to be deserved. They feel such love is too wonderful, too exotic to be owned by ordinary souls.

Such is our first love for Jesus. Many new converts awaken the morning after their conversion to euphoria. But there is another kind of reaction to grace. The morning after I first came to know his love, I awoke a little disappointed. What felt so adequate the night before seemed suddenly too small to trust. I knew I was one with Jesus in an imperishable union. But I wanted more of the bliss of grace to remain. The magic of my "delirium" seemed too soon gone. But why did I so treasure the warm feelings of first faith? Did this not make grace too gooey to have real substance? Was I not getting mushy—schmaltzy—with God? Wouldn't it be better to love God with good, hard theology minus giddy emotionalism? Perhaps, but who would want to love God without the ardor and the buoyancy of the poets?

G. K. Chesterton once spoke of the love of God as a romance. Who can deny it? It is a romance—a divine romance. This romance, said Chesterton, is deeper than reality.[2] What can he have meant by this? He meant that this reality can be measured only in my heart through the use of my inner and more hidden senses. I can measure some reality in miles or pounds or milligrams. But the love that goes deeper than reality is unquantifiable. It is heady, mysterious, immeasurable, elusive . . . and real.

"Jesus loves me" is unprovable but never open to much debate. Between the Genesis downbeat and the final chord of Revelation is a vast, unfolding song of love. God loves Adam and gives him a garden as a studio where he paints his love in bold, natural strokes. God loves Abraham and his love teaches us that barrenness and old age cannot thwart the gift of a child or the birth of nations. God loves Isaac, Jacob, Moses, David. And if this matter-of-fact tale of his love is not enough, he tells us plainly that he loved the world so much he gave us the gift of his son. God's great love is the grand essential of all worthy living.

What, then, can contain the expanding effervescence of God's love? Not our small hearts. You'd easier carry Gibraltar home in a marble bag. I remember the first joy of my romance with God. I came home after a revival service and told my mother, "Mama, somebody just found me!" The miracle is that I woke the next day to discover that my "foundness" was not a temporary euphoria—it was a way of life.

Jesus' love taught me that being found and being lost are categories of existence like health and illness. If you are one, you can't be the other. I knew that "lostness" was nothing more than ego forging into a woods without a compass. Further, I knew that "foundness" was a path to significance. It was essential, like the love of Christ itself.

Foundness is that state of being we feel when we believe ourselves to be winners in the game of life. What hides itself in the love of Christ that makes this so essential? First, it is necessary to remind ourselves that most human beings feel a natural hunger to win. God can make some use of this desire. But this desperate hunger causes us to want our own way and gives rise to a need to win. Eric Liddell, the missionary and running

champion of *Chariots of Fire*, confessed that when he ran
he "felt God's pleasure." But he also acknowledged that
the source of all our winning arises from the power
within us. "Jesus loves me" forms the syllables of
strength that tell me I am safe before the conflicts I
must face. Life is tough, but I can make it. I am loved!

Yet do I always win? No, not always. Sometimes—in
spite of love—I stand weak before battles that are
larger than I am. Even "clothed with Christ," I don't
always win.

When I first sampled grace, this inability to win over
every conflict left me unhappy. I learned with pain that
being found did not guarantee I would always win.
What a pain in our hearts—to have a new nature yet
always to carry about the old one. To be his and yet so
much myself, I would learn, was part of the human condition.

But our need to win must be placed beneath the
security of being loved that only Jesus can supply.
There is an old axiom that speaks of our double bias
for good and evil:

> *There is so much good in the worst of us*
> *And so much bad in the best of us,*
> *That it hardly behooves the most of us,*
> *To talk about the rest of us.*

There is a dark side to loving Christ. We are not as
steadfast in loving him as he is in loving us. Even
"sweet" little children who sing "Jesus Loves Me" can
display a rather frightening ability to be unloving.
Indeed, they can be cruel. Even the most devoted
people are not always Christlike.

DEALING WITH THE EGO
THAT DEVOURS US

When I was a pastor, a somewhat distraught mother in my church called me. Her little boy, she said, had quarreled all day long with his sister. They had not played well together and had come to slaps and blows over the various issues of their childish disagreements. Their fighting, she said, was evidence that, in spite of all her attempts to get them to be loving and kind, they were capable of instant cruelty. But her worst trial came at the time of their bedtime prayers when Christopher, her son, prayed, "God, please send a big dog to eat up Mandy." Fortunately for his sister, the boy's prayer carried little clout in heaven.

Where do little boys—beautiful, pure little boys—come up with such ungodly ideas? Russian author Alexander Solzhenitsyn observed that the line separating good and evil passes "not through states or political parties but through the center of every human heart." How nice and tidy it would be if we could honestly say, "Those evil people over there are not at all like us." Such sweeping generalizations are the basis of prejudice, but they are always dishonest.

I grew up during the horrible days of the Third Reich. In our little grade school we demonized Hitler as the distillation of all evil. We in Oklahoma were good by comparison. As we walked home from school in the early forties we would chant, "Step on a crack and you break Hitler's back." We worked hard to step on every crack we could. Hitler was German; Hitler was bad.

Then one day I realized we Millers were once Muellers. I too was German. I was the same nationality as Hitler. Was his evil in me? To some level, yes. It was only the degree to which we served it that was different.

While I wanted to critique little Christopher's prayer, I must confess that I have met some unlovely people myself. It sometimes makes me wish I kept a big dog to supplement my prayer life. But such dogs point up the horrible chasm between good and evil and how both are always present within all of us.

Do you remember the kindly Dr. Jekyll in Stevenson's novel? He began experimenting with his evil nature and ended up ruing the day he first summoned the monster within him. Jekyll, the gracious, caring physician, is at last only Henry Hyde, the night-stalker and murderer. It is a grisly parable of the final end of our double nature. Martin Luther put it well when he said we are all both "saint and sinner." How true!

We all must take seriously the sad lesson of Dr. Jekyll. The more we summon up the monster within us, the more we, like Dr. Jekyll, will find the monster unwilling to give up its control over our lives. Finally, all that is best about us will be captive to all that is worst about us.

But let us press the issue of this inner evil a bit further. What would have happened if God had actually answered Christopher's prayer and sent the dog to devour Mandy? Well, initially the world would have been quieter for Christopher. Since there is also a great deal of good in Christopher, he doubtless would have missed Mandy after her eulogy and memorial service. Then he likely would have wished her back.

But if the Stevenson parable holds, Christopher would also have kept the dog. Then, of course, when his mother displeased him, there would have been another sweet hour of prayer and another devouring. Each time someone displeased him, he would have summoned the dog. Since there are any number of adults who displease a child, one can only imagine how the dog would grow in Christopher's sociopathy. The teacher, the traffic cop, his camp counselor—all would exist merely to make him happy. Each time they didn't, they would drop out of his life and his dog would grow.

There is, however, an antidote to the big-dog mentality that tries to coexist with God's love.

THE ART OF LETTING GO

What most lovers seek is the return of their love. Every Romeo wants his ardor for his Juliet to be reflected. I was desperately in love at twenty-two years of age. Barbara was the central focus of my concentration. Her presence made all other love seem unimportant. We were openly affectionate. We embraced unapologetically on train platforms. We clung openly to each other at airports. At restaurants we picked at our food while talking and listening to each other's chatter with unbroken focus. While walking down a street I held Barbara's hand tightly as though unseen demons might leap from the dark shrubbery and rip us apart. We could not sit close enough in the theater. We felt contempt for the bucket seats that forced us to opposite sides of the divorcing gear-shift console of our automobile.

Our love knew one great value—being together. It knew but one fear—being torn apart. The strength of our ardor detached us from our smaller allegiances and unimportant schedules. We had voluntarily let go of all lesser concerns. We were in love.

In those days we marked the odd behavior of older, married couples—how little they seemed to need each other. They watched television while they ate, took separate vacations, and didn't like to crowd each other as they walked down a sidewalk. If he held her coat or pulled back her chair, she looked as though she suspected him of being up to something. What produced the difference between these two scenarios? Detachment.

The focus Barb and I felt for each other came as a result of our detachment—our letting go—from the dull world around us. We knew that the focus of our togetherness was only possible when we agreed to let go of the world at hand. Only then could we bask in the world we had created for ourselves. This was a world where we mattered. The closeness of our love came from our willingness to quit clinging to our separateness in favor of our togetherness.

I count it one of the richest experiences of my life to have been in Calcutta when Mother Teresa died. I was swept up in the city's adulation of this great woman. I always wondered why it was that she made such an impact on this largely Hindu city. I believe it was only because she had detached herself from all she had formerly desired. Because she had abandoned all self-interest, she could see the needs of her city. Otherwise she would have been blind to them. She confessed she had also detached herself from the masses to gain a person-by-person focus in Calcutta. Why had she impacted a city of twenty-two million? Precisely because she never quit seeing the city one person at a time:

I never look at the masses as my responsibility. I look only at the individual. I can love only one person at a time. I can feed only one person at a time. Just one, one, one. So you begin . . . I begin. I picked up one person—maybe if I didn't pick up that one person I wouldn't have picked up the others. The whole work is only a drop in the ocean. But if we don't put the drop in, the ocean would be one drop less. Same thing for you. Same thing in your family. Same thing in the church where you go. Just begin . . . one, one, one . . .[3]

One . . . one . . . one . . . This is how Jesus loves me. Who could be enthralled with a Jesus who loved every-body *en masse?* We love Christ only because he is able to love us one at a time. No wonder we call him our *personal* Savior. No wonder we sing "Jesus loves me" and never do we sing "Jesus loves the masses."

LETTING GO: THE KEY TO FOCUSED LOVE

But there is one other great advantage to loving Christ with a detached, single focus. It opens us up to see our world and enjoy it. Author Brent Curtis said that on his lonely walks in the country he would suddenly wake in the midst of "singers."[4] The voices of crickets and cicadas and katydids were a symphony unnoticed in larger crowds but much in abundance when he gained the ear of solitude and detachment. Donald Hudson called art "a window on heaven."[5] Only letting go of the world at hand can open such windows.

Jesus loves me: letting go of the busyness of my life does not cause Jesus to love me more, but it does free me up to discover and enjoy his love.

Once I let go of all things hurried, I can see the color and force of those treasures to be found in the love of God. Jesus loves me with sunrises, sunsets, spangled skies, and lonely gulls set against fields of burning blue.

His arms open in a vast, oceanic embrace to enfold me in wonder. It is a splendor that overwhelms me, a glory that engulfs me. It leaves me gawking at the ocean of his love, stupefied by its immensity and the smallness of my own needy soul.

But how is our letting go accomplished? How do we unhook from the frenetic busyness that occupies our lives? Perhaps the first step of letting go comes in realizing how important it is. One often gets the feeling that most people cherish their self-important pace. When they stop they can see that it is void of any real content. Still, they like the momentary frenzy if only because it gives them feelings of involvement and self-importance.

The courage to let go stands at the edge of our adrenaline-driven, shallow involvements. It rebukes us. Then all too often it turns its back on our frantic lifestyles and walks away. Walks where? Into a focused togetherness with Christ. Once we are alone with him, his love nourishes our solitude. Now we can see it! Having cleared the hurried clutter from our lives, we make room for our genuine friend, Jesus. He loves us, this we know. Our solitude brings us a new solidarity. It doesn't bring God to us; it brings us to him. He was there, loving us all the time. We just had to make a place in the middle of our busyness to see Him.

Psychologist Gerald May calls this letting go *detachment* and shows us just how important it is. *Detachment* describes not a freedom *of* desire but a freedom *from* desire. The real understanding of detachment "aims at correcting one's own anxious grasping in order to free oneself for a committed relationship to God."[6]

The late Catherine Marshall, author of the beloved *Christy,* used the word *relinquishment* in a similar way. *Relinquishment* is the difficult art of opening our grasp to let go of those appetites that trap us. The most fitting metaphor of this is a monkey trying to retrieve peanuts from a narrow-necked bottle. The monkey cannot retrieve the peanuts as long as he holds them in his fist, which will not pass through the bottle neck. Only if he relinquishes the peanuts can he ever be free.

In such a simple way we too are held captive by our wants and desires. Some of us are addicted to drugs or alcohol or sex or gambling. Others are addicted to reputation, style, or fame. But all of our drives must somewhere face our renunciation or they will send us to our graves.

Author Richard Foster reminded us in *Celebration of Discipline* that even the struggle to succeed may be an addiction. Many would-be disciples, says Foster, need to lay aside the heavy burden of getting ahead.[7] Our hand is trapped while grasping for more. Only in dropping everything can we be free. We cannot clutch at Jesus and the goodies of life with equal ardor and claim them both.

THE POWER OF LETTING GO

One of the hardest things to relinquish is our need to run things: power! We all seem to crave it at times. Why? It allows us to control others. But our appetite for power wars against Jesus' love. In desiring power, we are most unlike Jesus! Power would allow us to avenge ourselves on those who mistreat us. How differently Jesus handled this appetite. Should *we* ever stand before Pilate, we would want to see how *he* would look in a crown of thorns. Let us put Herod on the cross and ask him how *he* likes it.

Want power? Be careful! What horrors are bound up

in the power addiction. Don't think me too harsh in this matter, but let us take the worst dictator we can imagine: Pol Pot, Idi Amin, Saddam, or Adolph. One cannot help the feeling that somewhere along the line, they found Christopher's "big dog" solution to getting their way. Once they found how to get their way, the worst kind of evil marched across the face of the earth. So little Christopher's prayer really is something to be concerned about.

It is so easy to love the world and push it to make it yield all it will. We are all too prone to serve the hideous demon of power: *"I* must have this power, God." "How will this benefit *me?"* It is only Christ's cross that teaches us the glory of trading our power for his power. Then, filled with love, we cease crying "Mine, mine, mine" and begin crying "Yours, yours, yours! All is yours! Yours now and yours forever, God—yours, yours, yours!"

We break our addiction to power by relinquishing it. Thus we are kept from the perverted need to love ourselves. Thus the knowledge that Jesus loves me frees me from the fatiguing attempt to get the rest of the world to do it. Whether we serve Christ or ourselves makes a vast difference in how we end up in life. This difference can be as wide as the distance between Idi Amin and Mother Teresa. You may be sure that letting go of a lust for power was unknown to Idi Amin and yet it was the daily bread of Teresa of Calcutta.

Love keeps no big dogs. It wishes no enemy devoured. The apostle Paul set forth its virtues in this way: "Love is patient, love is kind. It does not envy, it does not boast, it is not proud. It is not rude, it is not self-seeking, it is not easily angered, it keeps no record of wrongs. Love does not delight in evil but rejoices with the truth. It always protects, always trusts, always hopes, always perseveres" (1 Cor. 13:4–7).

> *Is the night too cold, he is the fire.*
> *Is the mountain too high, he is the ascent.*
> *Are the days dark, he is the path.*
> *Is the night void of hope, he has come to spend the night.*

CONCLUSION

I am certain of this one thing: Jesus loves me, I can make it! I have found his love steadfast in every venture. I have claimed "Jesus loves me" as my musical testament. I rarely sing aloud, but for sixty years now its enabling melody has ricocheted through the corridors of my heart. No trial has silenced the song. No tempest has dulled the tune. Jesus loves me, I can make it. His love is my mode of survival, my liberation from myself, my way of triumph.

QUESTIONS FOR REFLECTION

1. Why do you think Chesterton implied that God's love of us was a "divine romance?"
2. What did Luther mean when he said we are at once both saint and sinner? How can we tell which of these two are in charge at any given moment? What can we do to be sure that, most of the time, the saint is running the show?
3. In what way does God's love release "the power within us"? What is the source of that power? Is it

available for every use? How can this power best be used?

4. What did Solzhenitsyn mean when he said that the line separating good and evil passed not through the center of parliament, but only through the center of individual human hearts?

5. Relate the art of loving God and the art of detachment. Which art do we serve first? Is this an important issue in developing a Christ-filled life?

6. In what way did Teresa of Calcutta simplify our individual calling when she said, "I can only feed one hungry person at a time"?

7. What do you think the author means when he encourages us to pursue "a symphony of solitude" if we are ever to understand the music of the kingdom of God? Can we serve God without this discipline?

8. What did Catherine Marshall mean by the word *relinquishment?* How can we use this discipline in our lives? Can we live effective Christian lives without it?

CHAPTER 2

Jesus Loves Me—He Is Creating a Better Me

Here is God the great enabler:

Oh, children of the Great King, let us pray that we may know the grandeur of our position before Him; the high calling with which we have been called; the vast responsibilities with which we are entrusted; the great work of co-operating with God in erecting the city of God. Heirs of God and joint-heirs with Christ! Called to sit with Christ in the Heavenlies! Risen, ascended, crowned in Him! Sitting with Christ, far above all principality and power! How can we go down—down to the world that rejected Him; down to the level of the first Adam, from which, at so great cost, we have been raised; down to the quarry from which we were hewn, and the hole of the pit whence we were digged! No, it cannot be; and as we make our choice, let us look to the living and ascended Christ to make it good. Put your will on his side, and expect that the energy of the power that raised Him from the dead will raise and maintain you in union with Him. For "your life is hid with Christ in God."

F. B. Meyer[1]

A CONVERSATION WITH JESUS

Lord I feel so weak today.

Let your weakness turn to me for strength. Have you not read the prophet Isaiah: "Come, all you who are thirsty, come to the waters; and you who have no money come, buy, and eat! Come, buy wine and milk without money and without cost."

Can your strength be so easy to obtain?

Let me breathe on you that you may receive the same power I once gave my disciples. They too were weak, yet they went forth clothed in my strength and returned to testify, "Lord, even the demons were subjected to us in the power of your name."

Oh Lord, I need that very power today . . . right now. Give it to me.

I will, for all who clothe themselves in my strength find my power rages through them. This power is yours. My Father has put all things beneath my feet as I now place all things under your feet.

So have I your assurance that I can enter my world and take charge of my circumstances?

You may be sure of that. As my love fills you, it will displace your weakness with my strength. Take charge of your world. I have given you authority to

trample snakes and scorpions. You shall overcome all
the power of the enemy. Nothing will harm you.
Rejoice not, however, that the spirits submit to you;
but rejoice that your names are written in heaven.

Isaiah 55:1; Luke 10:19–20

We are not asked to love God ardently while he pretends only a casual interest in us. He is furiously, passionately in love with us. "The unfathomable mystery of God is that God is a lover who wants to be loved," said Henri Nouwen.[2] Furthermore, this God is rather like a girl expecting a proposal: he is eager for the question.

The authors of *The Sacred Romance* tell us just how ardently our divine Lord pursues our love: he romances us with "creek-side singers and pastel sunsets, with the austere majesty of snowcapped mountains and the poignant flames of autumn colors."[3]

I am a lover of nature hikes who conceives of each walk as a *hajj*—a pilgrimage into his presence. Experience enables me to become the best I can be. I was raised by a single parent. I was not very old before I began to sense that this woman, my mother, had only one real reason to exist—me! Once I understood this I knew I would rather do anything than disappoint her love. She has been gone now for twenty-five years but her love over the last six decades has never ceased to summon me to be my very best self.

The summons to love is a call to honor. Jesus' love likewise summons up within us a sense of calling. When his love surrounds us, we discover who we are.

When I was in the sixth grade I saw the movie called *Trapeze*. I was entranced by the grace and courage of those flying trapeze artists. After leaving the movie I became convinced that God was calling me to be a trapeze artist. I hung some ropes in the trees and began my rehearsal for my life calling. I tried to convince my sister that God was also calling her and had some evangelistic success in recruiting her to become a part of the Flying Millers. But after I dropped her a time or two, she was somewhat insecure about either of our callings.

Then someone took a picture of me. When it was developed I could see that I was too lanky to begin my career. I needed more muscle. I began lifting weights, but my x-ray physique just wouldn't thicken to trapeze proportions. Finally I had to admit that no one saw my identity as I did. Most still saw me as a skinny sixth-grader; my identity as an aerialist was all in my mind.

Still, whom we hunger to be has a great deal to do with whom we become.

In the years since then, I have wanted to be more like Christ than Burt Lancaster, the star of *Trapeze*. Christ's love called me from circus mediocrity and summoned me toward things more excellent.

LOVE: THE IDENTITY OF JESUS

The further we move into understanding his love, the clearer becomes our understanding of our calling. The clearer we see what he wants, the surer we are of our identity. Our sense of identity causes us to read his purpose for our lives into everything we do.

How large is the testament of Jesus' love in the lives of all who have ever served him? The stone of fourteen-story cathedral altars cry his glory. Passion plays roll from Oberammergau, Austria. Music falls in symphonic cascades from the opera houses of the centuries. Yet even the grandeur of the Christ of the Andes or the Florentine Savior cannot speak with any greater eloquence than a single child singing the timeless tribute: "Jesus loves me! This I know."

Larry King, during a recent telecast, was asked, "If you had a chance to interview anybody throughout history, whom would you choose above all others?" He agreed it would be Jesus Christ. He said he would like to ask him, "Are you virgin born?" It seemed an odd question to me, but then King said, "The positive answer to that question would explain history to me."[4]

Why would the interviewer consider this question so pivotal? It seems to me that if King could know that this great miracle was true, then Christ, in his mind, would have to be all he claimed to be. In accepting this truth he would then have to face the love of Christ. He would be forced to accept Jesus' love or consent to live an irrelevant life.

Thomas the Apostle was rather like Larry King in some ways. He too had a problem with believing that was also a crisis in loving. With Thomas it was not the Virgin Birth that was so troubling. It was the Resurrection. Jesus had died. There was no doubt about it. Thomas was convinced that unless he saw Christ alive again and put his fingers into the nail prints and ran his hand into Jesus' spear-punctured side, he would not believe. Unlike Larry King, Thomas actually got his chance to interview Jesus. Thomas not only faced the living Christ, but also had to confess that he was the loving Christ. Jesus invited Thomas to thrust his fingers into his wounds to prove that the wounds were real, and thus to certify the miracle. It was most unsettling! But when the interview was over, Jesus said to this "seeing is believing" apostle, "Blessed are those who see and believe. But even more blessed are those who never having seen, still believe" (see John 20:29). Above the words "Jesus is alive" stands the words "Jesus loves you."

LOVE: THE BREAKFAST
OF CHAMPIONS

Og Mandino, in his book *The Greatest Salesman in the World*, tells the story of a great athlete who became confined to a wheelchair in his later years. He had a son, Tommy, who was not a great athlete but who in truth loved his father very much. His love for his father kept Tommy at the business of trying to be the best athlete he possibly could be. Still for all his effort, Tommy rarely finished well and often finished last. There was little that was sleek in his stride. His fellow athletes said he ran with a kind of waddle that was embarrassing to watch. But when each day's practice was over, Tommy would return to his father, who always said to him, "Don't give up, Tommy. Keep trying. Someday you are going to win a big race, and when you do, so help me God, I'm going to get up out of this wheelchair and walk."

Well, it happened that in the course of his life, the day finally came and before a huge crowd, Tommy finally won a big race. The crowd cheered and his Dad got up out of the wheelchair and walked.

There is much that sounds apocryphal about the story. Such boys are inevitably called Tommy or Billy or Sammy. But the point is we dare not quit telling these stories because they bear an incredible amount of "win one for the old gipper" kind of truth. Whom we long to be like tells us whom we are apt to become.

We do know that Derek Redman, after being hamstrung in the '92 Barcelona Olympics, inspired his watching father to come down from the stands and help his son stagger across the finish line. His son didn't win a big race, but he finished one . . . due to the love of his father.

One of my favorite friends was born in Eastern India. We once served in the same church. In the process of helping him get a green card, I gave him much counsel. But after receiving my help he became my associate pastor. How diligent his loyalty to me! My burdens every day were made lighter by his commitment. His gratitude and my gratitude came to bear on our common commitment to each other's welfare. Our bond grew because we both had the same identity goal: we wanted to be like Jesus. We spent endless hours talking about Christ, praying to Christ, and serving him in the hospitals and streets of our town.

The day came when my friend actually received his green card. That day was as splendid—and celebrated—for me as for him. He was on his way to U.S. citizenship and our church was indebted to his pilgrimage.

Love blesses those who give and those who receive it. Love sets us free of bogus feelings that we need to appear charitable. It is too great for such trivial pretense. I once asked a Korean student why he consistently led his class in making good grades. "I admire my father," he said. "He has made great sacrifices for me to come to America to study. I would be ashamed not to make good grades."

Once we understand the Father's love, we can look into the heavens and cry, "God, I would be ashamed to fail your love."

I was the first of my mother's nine children to go to college. During my years of study—week by week—I received three or four dollars cash (a wholesome, livable fund in 1954), which purchased such staples as soap and toothpaste. My mother had other children at home to support. She made only sixteen dollars per week and yet gave me a fourth of it. People do not make those kinds of sacrifices unless they are driven by the passion of their loving. Nearly fifty years have passed since then, but I have never forgotten her sacrifice. I cannot abandon my admiration for her.

It is also Christ's sacrifice for me that births in me a gratitude I cannot shake off.

LOVE: LOOKING LIKE CHRIST

It follows then that having Jesus as a role model means I must continually walk with him. Yet my lifelong commitment to this walk is never dull. When is love ever dull? When is romance mundane? Never! For I am always living in the midst of God's supply.

I am living in an all-you-can-eat restaurant, glutting on grace. I never leave the table. The banquet is forever. While I don't deserve the richness of his table, I never question its bounty. Jesus loves me abundantly, outrageously. I will never surrender my napkin and fork.

The country people in the part of Oklahoma where I was raised had a saying that the longer two people lived together, the more they looked like each other. I have mixed emotions about the proverb. Nothing, it would seem, can alter the skeletal structure of the face or the length of bones or sinews that might enable people to actually look alike. Still, I sometimes wonder.

I once knew an old missionary couple who gave me a perspective of identity with Christ. They had met in England during World War I. They came to America, received seminary training, and went to Argentina for the next forty years of their lives. There are several characteristics I will never forget about them.

First, they both loved Jesus.

Second, they prayed nearly all the time, and when they weren't actually talking to Jesus, they were talking about him.

Third, they went everywhere together, and having no car they usually walked. They each walked with the same rolling gait, as if they were joined at the hip.

But it was a fourth quality that made them most memorable: they were both intrigued by Jesus and this intrigue in some sense made them appear other-worldly. I had not known them for long before I began to sense that life had been very hard for them. Within the small circumference of their family they had dealt with debilitating disease and death. Their children had suffered much and they along with them. They had lived in isolated, lonely places—the furthest outposts of missionary work. For months at a time they were out of communication with anyone who might have given them help in time of need. But Jesus loved them and they him. Gradually the struggles of life and the hor-rors of death had brought them through seasons of weeping to Jesus, the Grand Supplier. In becoming like Jesus they had become like each other.

LOVE: THE END OF FEAR

There is one other attribute of Christ-identity. In his presence, we are unafraid. When we are with Christ, we are free from fear. "Jesus loves me" is the motivator of much noble courage in the human spirit. In Singapore recently I met a small woman in her early thirties who is a missionary to Indonesia. Islamization often requires a heavy price and the area of Indonesia where she lives is in constant political turmoil. Militant Muslim fundamentalists represent a daily threat to her very life. So many non-Muslims have perished in that part of the world. I wondered, in meeting her, if I would have the courage to face what she faces as a normal part of life.

Yet she is not morose. She is charming and a wonderful asset to every conversation. I touched her joy, and instantly I was ashamed of all that I've ever complained about. "Are you not afraid to serve where you do?" I asked.

"Afraid!" she laughed. "Not afraid. Only loved. I might fear for my life if I had not already given it away. It was worth little, I assure you, when compared to the life I received in the exchange. I gave away what I could only hold on to for a while in exchange for what would hold on to me forever. It's very freeing, you know. No, I am not afraid! Only loved!"

This is one of the great gifts of love—a freedom from fear. John testified that "perfect love drives out fear" (1 John 4:18). The psalmist said that even the valley of the shadow of death could not terrorize him because he knew the unforsaking presence of a loving shepherd.

Sometimes the thought of love freeing us from fear seems altogether too grand. As a child I was always afraid of the dark. I will never forget a panel of plywood at the end of my bed that was garishly wallpapered. This overbold pattern was full of huge, dark leaves and somber shadows. It seemed to me that Maurice Sendak's *Where the Wild Things Are* lived in that horrible panel of wallpaper. Things with slitted eyes hid in that dark jungle and I feared both to look (and not look) all night long.

There was but one deliverance that brought me much assurance from the wallpaper: the presence of my mother. If I could remember she loved me and was in the house with me, her love delivered me from fear. In fact, I sometimes marveled that the wallpaper held no terror for her. She was unafraid! When I counted on her love, I too became fearless.

Love dumps adrenaline into our cowardice and transforms it to holy boldness. Fear in some ways is the most pitiable of the emotions. But Christ has taught me that fear is a fiend easily defanged and declawed by our devotion to God. Love packages the trembling soul in confidence. Then we can see we are too much loved to be afraid of anything. Jesus is my titan companion. None dare threaten me in his towering presence. There, every terror is a sissy, every dread is chained.

LOVE: AN ANCHOR IN THE MIDST OF TURMOIL

In addition to conquering our fear, Christ's love offers us peace in the midst of turmoil. In a Philippine seminary where I was teaching, one of my Indonesian students had come to our school after Islamic warriors burned his church and home. His family was left without shelter or income. Further, these Muslim militants had ordered him out of the country and told him that if he ever came back he would be killed. They actually fixed a price on his head.

He was a man trapped between worlds. He could stay in the Philippines only until he finished his degree and then his visa would no longer be renewed. Ultimately he would have to return to Indonesia. There certain death awaited him.

"Aren't you afraid?" I asked.

"Yes," he confessed. "I don't know what I shall do." Then he stopped and changed the subject. "Prof, in

this paper you've assigned, would you prefer it be ref-
erenced by footnotes or endnotes?"

Suddenly I felt ashamed. Here I was in a part of the
world where churches were burned and pastors mur-
dered, and the best I could do was teach my students
good syntax and scholarly composition. Yet the day
held a lesson for me. The lesson was this: we cannot live
incessantly concerned about the monstrous terrors of
life. What my friend didn't say was that Jesus loved him.
The very knowledge of such a love had liberated him
with enough peace to sit in a circle of hungry lions and
enjoy his own lunch.

Jesus' love offers me the great stability of his moder-
ation. The Book of Acts says that Paul and Silas, having
been beaten and thrown in jail in Philippi, sang songs
at midnight. How, with their backs cut to ribbons,
could they sing at midnight? And what did they sing?
"Jesus Loves Me" hadn't been written yet, so it was
surely something else. But whether it was a psalm or
some other kind of praise, it was a song that in some
way celebrated Christ's steadfast love.

Foxe's Book of Martyrs tells of the state- and religion-
sponsored murders of many believers. What is remarkable is that many of them in dying actually sang, like
Paul and Silas in prison, in their moment of blood.
What stabilized them during their dying? It could only
have been their utter adoration of Christ. His love
inspired a worship so voracious it set their immediate
pain at a distance.

Can love do that? Can love banish suffering? So
many studies have proved that our mental attitude can
assuage physical pain. Norman Cousins said his bout
with cancer was subject to his positive mental attitude.
Laughter and dread, he said, made lousy bedfellows.
He astounded the world by laughing his way to health.

In my thirty-five years as a pastor I have noticed a definite correlation between love and suffering. Those who are loved handle pain better than those who aren't. I am no doctor, but I can see a correlation between love and the amount of morphine needed to deal with the horror of a screaming nervous system.

This must have enabled the martyrs to "reckon that the sufferings of this present time [are] not worthy [to be compared] with the glory which shall be" (Rom. 8:18 KJV). Such loving not only takes the pain out of living, it takes the pain out of dying. Because I am in love with Christ, I can anticipate this love in final union. There is an old hymn that has become my definition of the future: "Someday the silver cord will break, and I right then as now shall sing. But oh the joy when I awake within the palace of the king."[5]

This is exactly why the apostle Paul, in writing Romans, contrasted the smaller consequences of persecution with the chain-smashing grandeur of Christ's love. The scriptures declare:

I consider that our present sufferings are not worth comparing with the glory that will be revealed in us . . .
   As it is written:
    "For your sake we face death all day long;
    we are considered as sheep to be slaughtered."
   No, in all these things we are more than conquerors through him who loved us. For I am convinced that neither death nor life, neither angels nor demons, neither the present nor the future, nor any powers, neither height nor depth, nor anything else in all creation, will be able to separate us from the love of God that is in Christ Jesus our Lord. (Rom. 8:18, 36–39)

Such love wraps the hymns of martyrs in flames.

But most of us are neither apostles nor martyrs. We must ferret out his love amidst the most ordinary of days. So let's leave the grand examples of love and ask what his love means to us more ordinary souls. How does this love serve an ordinary mother who is three days behind on laundry? How does it work for an executive who knows his days are numbered because he's been caught in a corporate downsizing? In the matter of simple things, can Jesus' love be the great healer of all our anxieties. "He values not Christ at all, who does not value Christ above all," said Augustine. This love is most freeing in the midst of the hassle but it must ever be wholehearted. "They do not love Christ, who love anything more than Christ," said Puritan theologian Thomas Brooks.⁶ "I have a great need for Christ," said Charles Spurgeon, "and I have a great Christ for my needs."⁷

Jesus does not contrast my small affairs with those of the martyrs. Nor does he stop loving me just because I have small problems, like not being able to get my locker open or having my charge card rejected at the zoo. Living in his love replaces my petty neuroses with the same confidence the martyrs knew. God really is in charge. Jesus is the Christ of any crisis because he is the Christ of every crisis. It takes a load off.

And what is the load it primarily reduces? The risk of betrayal. Here is the ugly word that makes us so afraid to love: betrayal. Everyone more than a few years of age has known this anguish. At one time or other we have all given ourselves away in utter trust only to feel the sting of treachery.

A young girl of my acquaintance gave herself completely to a man, and I do mean completely. When he was through with her, he snapped his fingers in her face and told her to "get lost." The fullness of her love was stabbed with a betrayal from which she will never quite recover. But such abandonment causes us to ask, "Will I ever be unfaithful to Jesus? How much of Judas Iscariot lives in me? Did not Judas, after being loved by Jesus, snap his fingers in the face of the Almighty and say, 'Get lost!'?"

A favorite novella of mine has a sequence in which a fiend chases the hero through rainy alleys. Once he is safe inside his house, the hero calls his dearest friend for help. But the phone rings unanswered. His source of help is gone. Then fear grips his heart with icy fingers. He turns to the window to behold the fanged face of his pursuer. Now leering at him through the streaming glass is the face of that very friend he was summoning for help.

The parable is real enough to convince me that only the unceasing love of God can give me courage to risk myself in the art of loving others. Am I afraid of the risk? Not desperately. God risked everything at the cross to prove his love for me. Surely I can play by the same rule; the servant is not greater than his Lord.

CONCLUSION

Jesus loves me . . . therefore, I am set free of the egoistic need to love myself. I am called by his love to be better than I otherwise might have been. His love enables me to live confidently and not be afraid that the hassles of life will steal my joy. His love cures my jitters. But best of all its qualities is that having accepted his love, I am free to really love all those around me. There is a contemporary Christian hymn that goes: "I am loved, I am loved. I can risk loving you." The simple song states both the blessing and the woe of love. Love is wonderful for all the reasons I've stated. But as the song points out, it is also risky.

I have found that being loved is like dressing for the winter. I must clothe myself in God's warm love or I will not be able to survive the Arctic treachery of human loving. It is cold out there in the real world. We must not sally into this frigid world inadequately prepared for the winter. We must dress for this moral arctic we call earth. We must clothe ourselves for the gales of earth's frigid reality.

Remember the home you once knew? How many times every winter did your mother cry, "Don't go outside without your mittens"? Was she purposely trying to make your life miserable? Certainly not. She was interested in your survival.

When God calls out to us, "Love the Lord your God with all your heart" (Matt. 22:37), is he trying to make our lives miserable? No, he is just begging us to dress warmly for the human condition. He wants us to be clothed in the wonderful warming love of God.

There is but one sure recipe for survival: Jesus loves us. His love is as certain as daylight. Count on it! Enjoy!

QUESTIONS FOR REFLECTION

1. In the section titled "Love: The Breakfast of Champions," there are several instances that show how love releases a power within us. Can you think of a specific time in your own life when you felt such a release?

2. What was produced in the student's life when he said he made good grades because he admired his father? Can you remember any specific incident in

your life when the love of your family caused you to act in a specific and worthy manner?

3. What do you think the apostle John meant when he wrote, "Perfect love drives out fear?" Are there times in your life when your own love of someone made you unafraid to stand—at some personal risk—on their behalf?

4. In this chapter the question is asked, "Can love set pain at a distance?" Can it? Cite some concrete examples of when this worked for you or someone you know.

5. What does the statement "Love enables martyrs to sing at midnight" mean?

CHAPTER 3

This I Know: Embracing Certainty

I know not how God's wondrous grace,
To me he hath made known,
Nor, why unworthy Christ in love
Redeemed me for His own.

I know not how the Spirit moves,
Convincing men of sin,
Revealing Jesus thro' the Word,
Creating faith in Him.

I know not when my Lord may come
At night or noonday fair,
Nor if I'll walk the vale with Him
Or "meet him in the air."

But "I know whom, I have believed,
And am persuaded that He is able
To keep that which I've committed
Unto him against that day."

DANIEL W. WHITTLE

A CONVERSATION WITH JESUS

Is it possible, Lord Jesus, to really know that you exist?

All the meaning to be had in life is hidden in my reality. Why do you fondle your doubt when all it has ever given you is a sickness in your soul? See me as I am. I am the Bread come down from heaven. I am the Word that was there in the beginning, the Word that took on flesh to dwell among you.

But how can we know that you really are who you say you are?

Taste and see. Bread is not called a liar while it's being eaten. I tell you the truth: I am the Bread of Life. He who comes to me will never hunger; he who believes in me will never thirst.

But aren't you claiming too much, and aren't we believing too much, to say that we can know for sure you are God's Son?

Just what I have been claiming all along. I am Bread, man! When you have lifted me up, you will know that I am the one I claim to be. I have done nothing on my own. I speak just what the Father has taught me. I am who I say I am, but more than that, I exist for you.

But how can I know that for sure?

I will tell you how you can know I love you—I am the Good Shepherd who lays down his life for the sheep. The hired hand does not own the sheep, so when he sees a wolf coming, he abandons the herd. But I am the Good Shepherd, I know my sheep and they know me—I lay down my life for them.

I doubt no more that you are life.
Doubt flinches in the face of dread.
I thirst, give me yourself to drink.
I hunger first then reach for bread.

JOHN 1:1,14; 6:35; 8:25–27; 10:11–14

In an uncertain and sometimes cruel world, we have a certain pier in the froth and foam of our need. It is this: "Jesus loves me! This I know." The phrase is a wonderful gift from God. Life too is a gift from God. But at times it seems to be a white-elephant gift.

What is a white-elephant gift?

In ancient India it was customary for the rich to seek to ruin other wealthy people. Their means was to give the person they wished to destroy a white elephant. In Hindu thought, all elephants were sacred, but a white elephant—an albino—was considered an incarnation of one of the Hindu gods. Such a creature was therefore considered the most worthy of gifts. Indeed, a white elephant was a gift too excellent, too costly, to be refused.

But it was also the most useless of gifts because, while it was divine, the beast was considered too holy to be used for common labor. Because of its godlike status it had to be given the best of food and care. Thus a holy elephant became a constant financial drain on anyone who owned it. It couldn't be killed. It had to die of old age, and rarely was its owner lucky enough to see such an elephant die young. So it was commonly conceded that the best way to drive an enemy into bankruptcy was to give him a white elephant.

To be able to sing and believe "Jesus loves me! This I know" is our creed. When our lives go well, we exult, "It's great to be alive!" But in moments of despondency we groan, "Is this all there is?" It is hard to appreciate life when it's mistreating us. As one philosopher put it, "Life is sometimes like a man with a bad headache. He doesn't want to cut his head off, but it hurts him to keep it."

But why is life so hard? Could it be because we work so hard to stay in charge of it.

FAITH IN GOD'S FUTURE IS THE PARENT OF SELF-CONFIDENCE

God is in charge so we can relax. "Jesus loves me," is the benediction of the angels. I had rather risk with God than play it safe without him. Those who live in his confident love are free to live confidently.

In his Pulitzer Prize-winning book *Leadership* James McGregor Burns extols one of the great leaders of the twentieth century, Woodrow Wilson. Wilson worked tirelessly to found the League of Nations. He was vigorously opposed by many who discredited him. Most of the time he failed to bring his great ideas to pass. Later, when the United Nations was born, it was generally agreed that Wilson had achieved after his life what he had vainly struggled to achieve during it.

In Christ we do not struggle to be victorious, we struggle to belong to God. But more than that, we long to know what may be known that will add security to our lives. "Jesus loves me! This I know" compels us onward. The battle is ours, the outcome His.

Never having seen Wilson's struggle, Theodore Roosevelt also extolled that visionary stamina that results from knowing for sure we cannot fail. Roosevelt wrote in 1899:

It is not the critic who counts: not the man who points out how the strong man stumbled or where the doer of deeds could have done them better. The credit belongs to the man who is actually in the arena; whose face is marred by dust and sweat and blood; who strives valiantly; who errs, and comes short again and again, because there is no effort without error and shortcoming; who does actually try to do the deed; who knows the great enthusiasm, the great devotion and spends himself in a worthy cause; who at the worst, if he fails, at least fails while daring greatly. Far better it is to dare mighty things, to win glorious triumphs even though checkered by failure, than to rank with those poor spirits who neither enjoy nor suffer much because they live in the gray twilight that knows neither victory nor defeat.[1]

Having faith in God's future teaches me that when I know that Jesus loves me, I know who I am. It is said that when ancient soldiers ran into a soldier they didn't recognize, the intruder's life depended upon his knowing who he was and what his mission was. If he could not clearly state his name and purpose, he was put to death.

Some of the most miserable people I know have little confidence in God and therefore cannot clearly state why they are in the world.

To know Jesus loves us is to know why we live, and thus it endears us to God, who craves our dependency so much more than he admires our self-sufficiency. Why should I be surprised that God feels this way? If I walk into a nursery and discover two children, one of whom is playing and one of whom is crying, to which of these children am I more quickly drawn? To the hurting child, of course. It is even so with God.

But there is nothing that so clears our spiritual vision like growing older. The longer we live with "Jesus loves me! This I know," the more confident we become.

Long ago I fell in love with a seventeenth-century prayer, attributed to an anonymous elderly nun:

Lord, you know better than I know myself that I am growing older, and will some day be old. Keep me from getting talkative, and particularly from the fatal habit of thinking that I must say something on every subject and on every occasion.

Release me from craving to straighten out everybody's affairs. Make me thoughtful but not moody; helpful but not bossy. With my vast store of wisdom it seems a pity not to use it all, but you know, Lord, that I want a few friends at the end. Keep my mind from the recital of endless details—give me wings to come to the point.

I ask for grace enough to listen to the tales of others' pains. But seal my lips on my own aches and pains—they are increasing, and my love of rehearsing them is becoming sweeter as the years go by. Help me to endure them with patience.

I dare not ask for improved memory, but for a growing humility and a lessening cocksureness when my memory seems to clash with the memories of others. Teach me the glorious lesson that occasionally it is possible that I may be mistaken.

Keep me reasonably sweet. I do not want to be a saint—some of them are so hard to live with—but a sour old woman is one of the crowning works of the devil.

Give me the ability to see good things in unex-

pected places, and talents in unexpected people.
And give me, O Lord, the grace to tell them so.

Here is a woman not bent on her right to retirement just because she is older. She knows Jesus loves her, and this knowledge keeps her eyes fixed on the God who guarantees the future. Retirement is no time for copping out or dropping out. Once having seen, she dares not sit in a rocker and abandon that vision.

BEING SURE OF WHAT WE HOPE FOR

Hebrews 11:1 states the essence of vision. It defines faith as "being sure of what we hope for." It sounds a bit like double talk. Is it really possible to be sure of what we hope for?

It seems to me there are three steps to conquering the unknown territory of God's promises. First we enter into that area I call "I don't know if this is so, but oh how I wish it were." Next, we advance into "I believe, but Lord, help thou my unbelief." Finally we reach the stage known as "I can see—but through a glass darkly."

But are each of these phases really steps of knowing? Is "I don't know if this is so, but oh how I wish it were" really knowing? Yes. The first step of knowing anything is a longing after the knowledge.

Consider the second step: "I believe, but Lord, help thou my unbelief." It too is a longing after belief. It is a distinct advancement over the first step, for when I pray this prayer I advance into the foggy shoals of faith far enough that I can see that the ocean really is out there.

Finally I come to the place where I see it all—but

dimly, through a dull mirror. The mirror is smoked. I can see Jesus, but his exact form eludes me. So I set out in pursuit of his reality. I hold him. I touch him like Magdalene at Easter. He is alive and I long to tell the world he is. But when others demand, "Prove he's alive!" I weep at my inability. For his form flees from me. He is ever out ahead of me on the horizon of my heart, yet dim, dim, dim. Still, I know, and my knowing is my treasure. I stare into the dark glass and I see him. Now I am very sure.

But each of these steps into what may not be seen is a step taken beyond the early portals of childhood. Children are incredible believers and thus they sing "Jesus loves me! This I know" and they really do know it. It is only with the advancing of years that they become more doubtful. Why? Who can say? Maybe in having to shuck the Santa Claus myth, they come to deal seriously with the reality of Jesus. Just when they were making a little money on their baby teeth, wham! No Tooth Fairy! Just when they were enjoying marsh-mallow Peeps, blam! No Easter Bunny!

Then the real questions begin: No Rapunzel? No Cinderella? Maybe no Jesus?

Shedding the protective armor of their first fan-tasies, they come at last to the first faltering of faith—a crisis in knowing. "Jesus loves me! This I know." Know? But how can we know?

How can we be sure of God? Are we more likely to be sure of him when the sun is shining or when we are lan-guishing in the depths of our need? I believe God always shows himself in the midst of our dependency far sooner than in times of our abundance.

I have a very old friend with whom I once attended seminary. Early on he was a fervent Calvinist, sure that all that happened to him had been predestined. He later abandoned his confidence and became an atheist. Still, as chance—or predestination—would have it, he ultimately wound up in the same city where I lived. I was a pastor in that city and he was a philosophy professor at a big university there. One day, just after I had visited a dying woman in the hospital, he invited me to his home for tea and a heaping tray of mint cookies. As we sipped we ate and talked, I asked him how he as an atheist would have spoken to this needy, dying woman. He said he would probably have told her what I told her—how she must count on the love of Jesus and look to him for hope.

"But," I protested, "you don't believe that."

"No," he said, "but what I believe would be of no help to her in her time of need."

I reminded him that atheism is a congenial subject for philosophers in warm rooms with tea and mint cookies, but the icy blasts of reality finally call us to cling to the God of confident promises. Let us defend the child's hymn, "Jesus loves me! This I know."

I DON'T KNOW IF THIS IS SO, BUT OH HOW I WISH IT WERE

The philosopher Eric Hofer said that we human beings are incurable believers. We do seem to be created with a natural yen to believe. We seem also to have a natural tendency to hurt. Faith is one way of coping with the hurt of being human.

These latter years of my life have often been given to serving in missions. I have traveled over much of the world, meeting missionaries and listening to them as they recount their experiences with God. Are they victorious experiences? Not all of them. I have met missionaries who, in addition to finding "Jesus" an unwelcome word in the cultures they served, have lost children. Yet "Jesus loves me! This I know" is foundational to their struggles. Many of them have argued about their calling as they wept oceans away from dying parents they longed to be near.

But I have met very few who would say they are living pointless lives. I think the most vibrant missionaries I have met are medical doctors serving in lonely outposts of the Arab world. These great physicians and nurses are aware that even in winning a Moslem to Christ, they condemn their converts to ostracism and persecution—even martyrdom. One doctor said to me, "How do you think I feel in longing to lead people to Christ, knowing that the moment my patients receive Christ they face a life-and-death contempt in this culture?"

"It must seem pointless," I said to this kindly doctor.

"Pointless?" he said. "Rather this is the point of the Gospel—the cost and consequence of receiving Christ is the entire point of Luke 9:23: 'Take up your cross and follow me.'"

Christ is the point!

I think Hofer was right: we are all incurable believers. We want there to be a God! Even in our moments of doubt (and doubt is often just faith under stress), I never doubt pointlessly. When I must doubt, I doubt with longing. In some ways I am a child singing, "Jesus loves me, this I long to know." I am a child celebrating the "is-ness" of Jesus Christ as I go on about my life.

Consider how any child reckons with the truth of Christ. To a child, the pictures of Jesus in the family Bible are like the pictures of Grandma in the family album. Both are taken at face value. To doubt Jesus is to doubt Grandma. They are both equally reasonable realities. A young girl talks to Grandma on the phone and waits for her to come at Christmas. The girl also talks to Jesus at night and waits for him to come again, which the entire believable world of adults has assured her is going to happen.

The argument is done and finished.

"Jesus equals Grandma equals reality." My Grandma Kent lived in Vernon, Texas, and Jesus lived in heaven. Grandma came to see us every year and Jesus was coming to see us at an unexpected hour and only God knew exactly when.

Still, I envisioned those moments to be somewhat alike. When Grandma came, we children were always in the yard, peering down the long lane where Granny would approach. We could hardly wait. She had a Mary Poppins-like carpet bag and she always brought us myriad treats and gifts. She did come more often than Jesus but we expected each of them sooner or later to show up. We knew we would be made rich by their visits.

BEING SURE

Once you have made the leap, then you join those believing scholars who gathered in Nicea in A.D. 325 and agreed upon the creed:

> We believe in one God . . . and in one Lord Jesus Christ, the Word of God, God of God, Light of Light, Son only-begotten, Firstborn of all Creation . . . Who was made flesh for our salvation and lived among men, and suffered and rose again on the third day, and ascended to the

Father, who shall come again in glory to judge the
living and the dead.

Still, after having confessed his reality with so theological a vow, you will most likely snuggle into bed with the
simpler creed you keep with Grandma's picture: "Jesus
loves me! This I know."

Know?

Know is such a cocksure word. There are times when
we must know a thing before we declare it. For
example, "Dinner's ready!" There are other times
when we check out all of the facts before we make the
announcement—we hurry into the dining room to see
everyone seated and eating and then we also declare,
"Dinner's ready."

In either case the dinner is real and ready. The only
difference is that on the one hand, you study before
you announce and on the other hand you announce
before you study. Knowing there's a Jesus is like that.
Most of us who agree on the reality of Jesus have first
announced it and later thought it all through.

Consider these who first announced it to be true and
later studied it out: "If ever the divine appeared on
earth it was in the person of Christ," said Goethe. "Jesus
Christ is the condescension of divinity and the exhala-
tion of humanity," said theologian Phillips Brooks. "It
pleases the Father that all fullness would be in Christ,
therefore there is nothing but emptiness anywhere
else," said William Gadsby.[2] Did all of these brilliant
thinkers arrive at these proclamations on the basis of
their brilliance? No, but their conclusion is an evidence
of their brilliance. They knew, experienced, ate, and
declared the dinner real.

Yet at some point reality must be tasted. The reality
of ice cream can be settled only by the tasting. But let

us say that in regard to ice cream, I deny certain of my senses in the matter. Let us say I first eat ice cream in the dark. I taste its glorious reality, but am unable to see it. So I proclaim the truth of ice cream on the basis of what I have only tried with one of my senses. Still, having partially experienced it, I am confident that in better light it might be seen and thus apprehended with more of my senses.

In the case of faith, longing for something to be true will bring us at last to the state of declaring it so. "Jesus loves me! This I know" may be ice cream at last proclaimed in the light after having first tasted it in the dark. Jesus is real. Our passion declares it.

CONCLUSION

Jesus loves me. This I know. The medieval writer, Julian of Norwich, once wrote:

> In spite of our poor choices and spiritual blindness in this life, our courteous Lord continues to love us. We will bring him the most pleasure if we rejoice with him and in him.
>
> When the end comes and we are taken for judgment above, we will then clearly understand in God the mysteries that puzzle us now. Not one of us will think to say, "Lord, if it had been some other way, all would be well."
>
> We shall all say in unison, "Lord, bless you because it is all the way it is. It is well. Now we can honestly see that everything is done as you intended; you planned it before anything was ever made."

What is the meaning of it all? Listen carefully.

Love is the Lord's meaning. Who reveals it? Love. Why does he reveal it? For love.

This is the only lesson there is. You will never learn another. Never. We began in love, and we shall see all of this in God forever.

QUESTIONS FOR REFLECTION

1. What does it mean to be a "*Britannica* believer"?
2. What did Theodore Roosevelt mean when he said, "It is not the critic who counts . . . [but] the man who is actually in the arena"? Have you ever faced criticism from someone who you felt didn't understand your battles? How did you handle it?
3. What does this statement mean: "Faith in God's future teaches me that God is knowable." Why is it so critically important to have our own individual mission statement? What can it mean to say we know why we are in the world? In what ways does this free up our lives to enjoy living?
4. What does the author mean when he says, "Once their humanity is gone, [people] pursue inhuman goals with inhumane zeal?" Can you think of someone on the international scene who has done this? Can you think of someone on a personal level who has done this? How, in either case, did the person's behavior change?
5. Tell how you felt about the prayer of the aging woman. How has your own aging process helped you to see more clearly the course of this world and your own part in it?
6. What does the statement "The child, in singing 'Jesus Loves Me,' has surpassed all theological argument and debate about the reality of Christ" mean?

CHAPTER 4

This I Know: Erasing Doubt

Starting very early, life has taught all of us to ignore and distrust the deepest yearnings of our heart. Life, for the most part, teaches us to suppress our longing and live only in the external world where efficiency and performance are everything. We have learned from parents and peers, at school, at work, and even from our spiritual mentors that something else is wanted from us other than our heart, which is to say, that which is most deeply *us*. Very seldom are we ever invited to live out of our heart. If we are wanted, we are often wanted for what we can offer functionally. If rich, we are honored for our wealth; if beautiful, for our looks, if intelligent, for our brains. So we learn to offer only those parts of us that are approved, living out a carefully crafted performance to gain acceptance from those who represent life to us. We divorce ourselves from our heart and begin to live a double life . . . For what shall we do when we wake one day to find we have lost touch with our heart and with it the very refuge where God's presence resides?

BRENT CURTIS AND JOHN ELDREDGE[1]

A CONVERSATION WITH JESUS

How can I be sure you know me?

Are you not one of my sheep? Am I not your shepherd?

My sheep hear my voice, and I know them and they follow me. I give unto them eternal life and they will never perish. My Father has made you a present unto me and no one can take you out of my Father's hand.

Why is it that even after you tell me you love me, I still doubt?

It is because you do not practice believing. Faith is an art. Its excellence depends on its exercise. Its quality derives from its discipline. Therefore practice believing until you believe. He who believes in me, though he were dead yet shall he live and all who believe in me will never die.

I do believe and yet I'm unsure. I want to really know, not merely believe.

Blessed are those who have seen and believe but more blessed are those who never having seen still live free of doubt.

Show me how I can know beyond all doubt.

Bring your little soul against my mighty acts. Consider who I am and doubt no more. Remember my response to Job?

Brace yourself like a man;
I will question you,
and you shall answer me.
Where were you when I laid the earth's foundation?
Tell me, if you understand.
Who marked off its dimensions?
Surely you know!
Who stretched a measuring line across it?
On what were its footings set,
or who laid its cornerstone—
while the morning stars sang together
and all the angels shouted for joy?

I have loved you with an everlasting love. Know whom you have believed, for I am able to forgive every sin you've ever committed.

2 TIMOTHY 1:12; JOB 38:3–7; JOHN 10:27–30; JOHN 11:25

Do we claim too much to say "Jesus loves me! This I know"? Certainly not. To know God is to know every thing that matters. But knowing God has built into it an odd inconsistency. How shall we small creatures ever know the vastness of our creator? Can our little legs ever keep up with him who strides the galaxies? Can our parochial ignorance ever span the cosmic mind of God?

Knowing we are loved by God is certain. Knowing anything else may be tenuous. In the fall of 2000 an astronomer discovered a new planet between Neptune and Pluto. It is not a large planet, only about one-eighth the size of Earth. This little world was quickly dubbed Plutino after its nearest neighbor. Most astronomers thought it to be no major discovery and their judgment seems worthy. Still, I must confess that the discovery provoked in me a kind of resentment of those truths I had been taught. My science books and grade-school teachers had all assured me there were only nine planets. Now I had to adjust my learning. What I once knew had to be amended in favor of a tenth planet.

How unsettling it is to have to adjust our knowledge. When all of human learning seems so transitory, how can we ever be sure that what we have learned of Christ will never need amendment? First faith is always exhil-arating. Believing for the first time is the reveille that wakens our souls to faith. We are excited to find that what we really wished was true is true. Jesus is alive! He loves us. And we know it. We have entered into Easter.

The sun is up—nay, the Son is up! Now that death is passé, our faith is triumphant. We are so buoyant in the glare of Easter joy that we wonder why we ever lived so long doubting it.

But sooner or later Easter Sunday passes. Monday arrives! The distant form of the Son of God seems less visible. He is still there. We are assured of this. But he is hidden by the workaday haze that obscures the bright form he so recently held. By Tuesday even Monday's bright, obscuring cloud has lost its lustre. By Wednesday the cloud is gone. Thursday we cry out for Jesus—all bright and beautiful—to be back with us. Friday finally comes. Alas, not Jesus. If we sing "This I know," we sing it all too faintly.

When Jesus will not show his face, there is born the desolate cry, "Lord, I believe. Help thou my unbelief." At such times I begin to realize the edge that the apostles held over me. They could actually see Jesus. They watched him stroll the Sea of Galilee and raise the dead. Like my peers I long for the back-then Jesus to become the right-now Jesus. In always having him, the apostles seemed to have it so much better than I do. But the reality is I can't find my way back to the place of victory. I cannot find the open, empty tomb. Life is too desperate. I need him and he is nowhere to be found. Alas, I feel a deadness at the center of my soul.

At such times I begin to lament with Louis Evely, the Dutch priest and lover of God:

> *If we'd lived in his day, if we could have heard*
> *   and seen*
> *   and touched Him,*
> *how dearly we'd have loved him.*
> *How gladly we'd have left everything to follow him.*[2]

If he hides himself for a long time I begin to doubt the creeds and wonder about the Scripture. How can I be sure that the apostles really saw him? How can anyone sing "This I know"? Isn't it only froth and arrogance? Why should I so glibly believe that they are telling me the whole truth?

"Jesus," I cry, "hide yourself no more! Let's all meet back at the open tomb. There we shall sit and enjoy once more the first light of Easter. There, in confidence we shall camp out in the wonder of joyous knowing and trusting."

THE HUNGER THAT CERTIFIES REALITY

One evidence that Jesus really exists is our hunger for him to exist. Author Malcolm Muggeridge said that our hunger for Christ tells us he is real even when we can't see him. He bases this certainty on the metaphor of our appetite. How? Well, our hunger for food tells us that food is real even when no food is visible. Muggeridge finally came to believe in the Christ he so long had doubted. He said the trip was more certain than he thought. Why? Because over the chasm of all his doubts there lay . . .

a cable bridge, frail, swaying, but passable. And this bridge, this reconciliation between the black despair of lying bound and gagged in the tiny dungeon of ego, and soaring upward into the white radiance of God's universal love—this bridge was the Incarnation, whose truth expresses that of the desperate need it meets. Because of our physical hunger we know there is bread.

Because of our spiritual hunger, we know there is Christ.[3]

In the same way my desperate desire to believe stands as an evidence that what I want to believe is true already. But isn't such a viewpoint at best naive? Wouldn't a child, by the same logic, wanting desperately to believe there was a Santa Claus, immediately guarantee his reality?

Of course. The difference is this: maturity. A child wanting there to be a Santa Claus has not tried all of the difficulties of logic on the "Santa proposition." Does the jolly old elf really live at the North Pole? There, where subzero temperatures prohibit nearly all life, could he really have his workshop? With so many children in the world, could he possibly get around to them all in a single night with eight very fatigued reindeer? Then there's the problem of chimneyless homes and the unexplainable cloning of his presence in a million December department stores. It is precisely this kind of logical testing that teaches children at last to deny him and to go on without him for the rest of their lives. The existence of Santa just can't stand up to the test of mature scrutiny.

Not so with knowing Jesus and his love. When we apply the test of hard scrutiny, he fares very well. Any of the martyrs will suffice to illustrate. People will die for a lie. Many have. But no one would die for a lie he or she knew was a lie. So far Santa Claus has no recordable martyrs. We know of no one who, when ordered to give up their faith in Santa, burned a pinch of incense to Nicholas. We have thousands of instances of believers doing just that in defense of their faith in Jesus. They died at flaming stakes, singing hymns with sentiments rather like "Jesus loves me! This I know." We have no instance of anyone dying while nailed to a Yule log, singing carols in defense of the Christmas elf.

Our nagging doubts about the reality of Jesus are erased when we meet those whose lives are lived for Christ under the most severe of challenges. I used to think how easy it would be to believe in the resurrection, if only someone had been at the tomb with a camera to take an actual photograph of Jesus walking out. But now I know photographs can be doctored. They are not the proof that I once thought they were. At an MGM Emporium I had a photographer take a picture of my head on Sylvester Stallone's body. It looks like me, and almost everyone says that I look better in that photo than I do in those where my head is on my own sagging form. This photo in some sense tells a flattering lie, but it lies. There are few proofs for any reality that cannot be doctored. So, if you would believe in the living Christ and not be disappointed, you must seek his reality in the life of someone who daily proves Christ real by single-minded faith.

THE CALCUTTA CONSTANT

I saw Mother Teresa only once. It was as she was lying in state in the Church of Saint Thomas in Calcutta. The memory of this encounter will be with me for the rest of my life. I did not see a dead saint lying in that church, but a living one. She gave almost four decades of her life to the "City of Joy" that to most Westerners is an endless wasteland of the dead and dying. Yet she went into the necropolis of Calcutta with life. Why? There is only one reason. Jesus was real to her.

When I saw her lying in state in the church I remembered something she once said when she was speaking to a group of married people:

> "Husbands, smile at your wives: wives, smile at your husbands and your children." They could not understand how I was able to tell them this sort of thing. "Are you married?" one of them asked. "Yes," I replied, "and sometimes I find it hard to smile at Jesus because he can be so demanding." And it is true. By our vow of chastity we are married to Jesus.[4]

In looking at her lifeless body, I remembered her vow of chastity to Christ and I recalled that in reality, she and Jesus had a marriage of forty years. Surely in examining such a long relationship, no one would doubt the existence of the groom. In fact, just seeing Mother Teresa called to mind how her confidence in Christ—her Groom—was evidence of his existence. If I needed more evidence, all I had to do was think of how the city itself had changed under the influence of her unwavering confidence in his reality. Because Jesus was so real to her, he became a good bit more real to the rest of us.

Seeing Mother Teresa's body called to remembrance an experience I had one day when traveling across the United States by air. I was seated next to an old nun. She was most congenial as she looked at my wedding ring and said, "Just how long have you been married, young man?"

I felt her question a bit abrupt but I answered, "Forty years."

Then she showed me her old, wrinkled hand, which sported a small, gold band. "I have been married for more than forty years to my Lord," she said.

I cannot escape the intrigue of such declarations. However non-Catholics greet such vows of celibacy, no one can doubt that such women are in love with Christ. I have wondered many times since then if, when Mother Teresa died, Christ must have felt himself a Widower. Heaven must consider the kind of love Teresa of Calcutta gave Christ as the richest of treasure. But I, for one, in visiting her houses for the dying, and seeing her godly influence in a needy world, was forced to cry, "He lives!"

In ministering to the sick and dying, Teresa said she was only "loving the disguised Christ." This was how Christ came to her, masked as suffering souls. No wonder she prayed:

> Dear Lord, may I see you today and every day in the presence of your sick, and whilst nursing them, minister unto you. Though you hide yourself behind the unattractive disguise of the irritable, the exacting, the unreasonable, may I still recognize you, and say, "Jesus, my patient, how sweet it is to serve you" . . . Oh, beloved sick, how doubly dear you are to me, when you personify Christ; and what a privilege is mine to be allowed to tend you. Sweetest Lord, make me appreciative of the dignity of my high vocation, and its many responsibilities. Never permit me to disgrace it, by giving way to coldness, unkindness or impatience . . . Lord, increase my faith, bless my efforts and work, now and forevermore, Amen.[5]

What I find most intriguing about Teresa's prayer is that after such wholehearted endorsements of the reality of God, she openly pleaded, "Lord, increase my faith." Is it possible that Teresa did not have all the faith she wanted? Yes. Is it possible that after dying so unreservedly for Christ in a foreign place, having turned a city of twenty-two million to Christ, she had doubts? Yes. After being married to Christ for so long, did she actually doubt the Bridegroom? Yes.

None of us has all the faith we want. But Calcutta held a lesson for me. Teresa's hunger for Christ was insatiable, but it was such a hunger that denoted the existence of food. It is never wrong to doubt food, but it is wrong to starve to death in a world of abundance. So it is with Jesus. It is never wrong to doubt him, only wrong to abandon all faith while his abundance of hope thrives in the world.

Isn't it wonderful that Jesus came to make the invisible God more visible? Yet his coming as God, to live as a mere man is not everywhere believed. Few real atheists exist. If you say, "God lives!" you will have almost none who argue. But what happens when you cry, "Christ is God and once stood physically on this planet?" Many will scoff at the notion that the great invisible, intangible God once became a man. The British philosopher Norman Kemp Smith spoke for many who doubt Christ when he said, "I have no difficulty with the idea of God, but I do with that of Christ: One time, one place, very difficult."[6] It is difficult for many to believe that God became a man and voluntarily entered the human arena.

Yet author and theologian Timothy George esteems this hard-to-believe event: "In the Incarnation, God the Son became flesh and blood, that part of the human person that is most vulnerable, most susceptible to suffering, decay, and death. Jesus was no phantom but truly human—of the same reality as we are."[7]

It is knowing this that sets us free and erases doubt— that gives us confidence we are loved. Knowing that gives us the certainty to sing, "Jesus loves me! This I know."

HOPE IN A DARK GLASS

Paul experienced a clear visitation of Jesus on the Damascus road (see Acts 9). Yet a number of years later he confessed, "Now we see but a poor reflection as in a mirror" (1 Cor. 13:12) or as the King James Bible says, "through a glass, darkly." In this world we are doomed to a poor perception of the next. It is said that when Parker Pillsbury attended the dying Emerson, he pushed his friend to tell him what he was seeing as he departed this life. He clearly hoped that Emerson would be able to give him some inkling of what heaven looked like as he approached it from his last earthly beachhead. "Can you see where you are going, Ralph? What does it look like over there?" Ralph, too fatigued to be very energetic in his response, replied, "Please, one world at a time, Parker. One world at a time."

Oz creator Frank Baum has Dorothy lament, "I don't think we're in Kansas anymore, Toto." Oz is always in the universe next door. We can't be in both worlds at once any more than we can be in Spain and Singapore at the same time. The reflections of the next world that we would so like to see can only be glimpsed in the poor mirror of the here and now.

Let us explore this dark glass.

Our current worldview of the world on the way is like our reflection in a comic, fun-house mirror. What we see in such a mirror is ourselves, but the image is at best distorted reality. It is us, yet not us. We are too thin, too fat, too everlastingly tall, too horribly and grotesquely squat. Is the reflection us? Yes . . . no. Yes, but in a poor mirror.

Paul said eternity is real, but temporarily the visibility is bad. Now it is only a dark, smoky mirror. The future is defined but we argue with the definition. The reflection of all we wanted to see is coated with scientism, secular grime, and soul abuse. The thousand arguments we have read of the atheists, of the agnostics, have put a film on the glass of our reason. Our years of doubt have smudged the mirror. Yet there is something there: a dim outline of the Christ the skeptical world has all but obscured. But what we can see we cherish. This dull glimpse is the focus of our adoration. But more than this, it strengthens our knowledge of his love.

That's what worship is for. On Sunday we bring our dull visions to the same joyous place. We come together to put together our partial visions. Then our obscure destiny begins to emerge in the bright light of our praise. We adore him. A picture emerges. The picture was there all the time; we just never had the joint perspective from which to view it.

Maria Pecche, like so many, was fascinated by a series of strange lines made by the Nazca Indians in the plains of Peru. Some of these odd lines covered many square miles. They were a baffling puzzle thought by many to be but ancient irrigation ditches. Then in 1939 Pecche flew over the area and discovered these baffling ditches were not ditches at all but drawings in the earth—pictures of birds and animals and insects.[8] In a similar way a bit of Windex on grimy glass furnishes us a clear picture of all things hidden. Jesus is real. We have the perspective; he can be seen. He loves us—we know it beyond all doubt!

Author Fyodor Dostoyevsky has one of the Brothers Karamazov say:

I believe there is nothing lovelier, deeper, more sympathetic and more perfect than the Saviour; I say to myself with jealous love that not only is there no one else like him, but that there could be no one. I would even say more. If any one could prove to me that Christ is outside the truth, and if the truth really did exclude Christ, I should prefer to stay with Christ and not with truth. There is in the world only one figure of absolute beauty: Christ. That infinitely lovely figure is as a matter of course an infinite marvel.[9]

In the smoky mirror, Dostoyevsky had seen enough to know that in a better mirror he would have seen it all. Yet as bad as the mirror is, it is the best glimpse possible. I can have this glimpse only when I have grown out of my doubting immaturity in Christ. Enoch suggested that when the smoky view of Christ clears we will "see the Son of Man sitting on the throne of his glory" (Enoch 62:5).

John confessed that when Christ came to him on the Isle of Patmos and he actually saw him clearly, he "fell at his feet as though dead" (Rev. 1:17). Sometimes we long for a clear view of Christ which in reality is a sight so terrible it would destroy us. We may be better off to study him in smoky mirrors and wait till we are granted the strength to see him "face to face," as the apostle Paul did (1 Cor. 13:12). But for now I have enough of this image to know that he exists. The smoky mirror bears witness while I wait for a better glass. Jesus loves me, this I know.

CONCLUSION

Doubt holds a latent blessing. It raises within us a certain coping madness. Most of us will do anything to keep from being disappointed. Yet believing with all our hearts sets us up for such disappointment. So, to avoid the let-down we don't give ourselves too completely lest our gullibility prove us fools.

Think of the childish tricks to which we have proved ourselves too gullible. Remember when some trickster, extending a deck of cards, said to you, "Have you ever played Fifty-Two Pickup?" When you confessed you hadn't, he sprayed your body with the cards, crying, "There're fifty-two of them! Pick 'em up!" He—and perhaps others—laughed uproariously as your face turned beet red. You had answered what appeared to be a sincere question and were laughed at as though you were a fool! So you armed yourself against such tricksters by being more cautious with your trust.

Deep in our hearts, we are always afraid that just when we've finished sincerely singing "Jesus Loves Me" someone will laugh in our face, shatter all our illusions, and cry, "Surprise! Only kidding! Jesus doesn't love you! You are on your own! Get honest and get real! You have no Father in heaven! God has a small, select roster of friends! You didn't make the list."

Of course that will never happen, but often so many of our good deals have gone bad that it is safer not to believe too much lest God or our pastor should be playing Fifty-Two Pickup with our souls.

Author Philip Yancey says that such humiliation of honest belief always arms us with doubt. He tells us about the children of alcoholics who survive their dysfunctional setting by saying to themselves, "Don't talk, don't trust, and don't feel." Christian counselors tell us that troubled Christians tend to operate by the same rules in relating to God. Emerging from a strict upbringing, or feeling disillusioned by some aspect of the Christian life, they squelch passion and fall back on a guarded, cautious faith.[10]

This is exactly what we must not do if we would lead victorious lives. We must wholeheartedly accept the realities of faith.

Even as a child I knew I could never cease loving Christ once I had embarked on the journey past the cross. I saw him come again and again to the destroyed souls around me, and the certainty of his love changed the battlefields of my life to playgrounds of joy. Jesus does indeed love me. I know it. Now I fearlessly believe two things: in his love anything is possible and all things are certain.

QUESTIONS FOR REFLECTION

1. What does the phrase "First faith is always exhilarating" mean? Do you remember the first steps of faith you took toward Christ? In what ways did you find them exhilarating?
2. What does the phrase "Lord, I believe, help thou my unbelief" mean?
3. What did Malcolm Muggeridge mean when he said, "Because of our physical hunger we know there is bread. Because of our spiritual hunger we know there is Christ"?
4. What does this statement mean to you: "There are few proofs for any reality that cannot be doctored."
5. What did Teresa of Calcutta mean when she said that in treating the sick and dying, she was treating the "disguised Christ"? Contrast this with the parable

Jesus told in Matthew 25:31–46. When did you last
actually use this parable as the scriptural justification
for your own service to Christ or his church? How
did you feel about it at the time? How do you feel
about it now?

6. What do you think is the real meaning of "through a
glass darkly"? Can you think of a needy time
when you wished for a clearer vision of Christ, but
found yourself relying on images in darker glass?
How did you reconcile this obscurity and fashion it
into confidence?

7. Is it true that believing with all our hearts sets us up
for massive disappointment? How are we to avoid
these times of disappointment? Are we to believe less
and use more skeptical judgment? Are we to trust
even more wholeheartedly in the future?

CHAPTER 5

For the Bible Tells Me So

Sing! God has a stylus in his hand.
He shouts in quill and ink,
"Here I am!"
Within this Book,
This Book of books,
This word incomparable,
This vellum currency
Surpassing excellence—
This scroll majestic.
In this Book I come,
Whispering in ink,
Breathing,
Revealing,
Disclosing,
Never Quitting!

Our God is literate!
Our God can write!
He lifts his starry quill
And the ages beg for paper!
A thousand pages of Adam's sad biography,
And on each one,
The grace-drawn portrait of his Son.

CALVIN MILLER

A CONVERSATION WITH JESUS

Jesus, how are we to feel about the scriptures? Are they trustworthy?

Yes, they are God's witness to himself, all in sweet accord within his triune being. The Scriptures cannot be broken.

Never?

No, not an iota nor a dot will pass from the Law till all is accomplished. No words were ever so unbreakable, so essential, so eternal.

But shouldn't modern thinkers such as ourselves reinterpret the scriptures to go more with our own day?

I say to you, *"Gegraptai!"* which means "It stands written!" The Word of God cannot be broken.

How did you handle those who refuse to have respect for the truth of the Bible?

I called them "foolish men" who were slow to believe all that the prophets had spoken! Now I command all later thinkers to reckon with the truth that knows no error and speaks in purity to all generations.

How did you find your own purposes for coming?

Rooted in Scripture was God's plan for my earthly sojourn. Beginning with Moses and all the prophets, I interpreted from the Scriptures things concerning myself. Now you must read yourself into these pages. Then you will know who you are and why you are here.

JOHN 10:35; MATTHEW 5:18; LUKE 18:31; LUKE 24:25–27

The Bible is God's diary, his last will and testament, his autobiography, his tied and bundled sheaf of love letters to the human race. It was written over fifteen hundred years of time while empires were forged. Its authors were alternately poets and convicts, adulterers and mystics. Yet I go again and again to these diverse writers to feast on their words of God. Why? I find that each time I open this book I set a hearing aid on my heart. Then I listen while the harsh gales of Sinai and the soft breezes of Galilee blow once again.

FOR THE BIBLE TELLS ME SO

I read and God speaks. I can hear him above the traffic of my hassled ways. Jesus is in this book, and I must read it to meet with him. I must read it to walk with him and to live a life that can matter to me only because it matters to him.

In recent years Western civilization has increasingly ignored this book. This is to our sorrow, for as Abraham Lincoln once said of the Bible:

In regard to this great book, I have but to say, it is the best gift God has given to man. All the good Savior gave to the world was communicated through this book. But for it we could not know right from wrong. All things most desirable for man's welfare, here and hereafter, are to be found portrayed in it.

The Bible's power to create and redeem us has existed historically in creating and redeeming cultures. The Bible is a simple book to comprehend. "Jesus loves me! This I know, for the Bible tells me so" is a simple, honest statement of our confidence in the Book. To its great credit it is as easily understood by plowboys as by princes. To some degree plowboys have been better than princes at reading it.

The Bible is the inspired Word of God. It is God's Book written by the most ordinary of souls to tell the world who God is and what he requires of it. God might have written the book in some uppity fashion that would remind the world he is very intelligent. But then only the intelligent would read his book and pay any attention to him. Jesus loves us—we know it!—the Bible tells us so.

A SIMPLE WORD FROM GOD

Fortunately for us less intelligent ones God wanted a wider audience—an audience less elite, more universally needy. The Bible didn't come to us by the same route as the literary classics came. The writings of some of the classic philosophers are older than the New Testament, but they were written in a literary language that once required a knowledge of classical Greek to understand. They still require a literary understanding of English. Not so with the New Testament. The books of the New Testament are written in a down-home kind of language called *Koine* or "street Greek."

Why did God keep this book so simple? He wanted it

to inform us of his love for us. He wanted to bring alive for the masses that simple line from "Jesus Loves Me": "Jesus loves me! This I know, for the Bible tells me so."

In the fourth century, when Jerome decided to translate the Bible from Greek into Latin, he translated it not in the style of such classic Roman writers as Cicero or Ovid. He translated the Bible's street Greek into Vulgate or street Latin. Does all this "street language" define the Bible as less worthy of literary merit than the works of the other contemporary writers of the time? Certainly not! God created a Book that would exist for the rank-and-file world, most of whom would never aspire to the classics.

It is odd that this simple book should have inspired great centers of learning. Scholars across the ages have met in ivied towers to wrangle through how this book was to be translated and interpreted. Across the centuries scholars have debated and dissected the Bible in their attempts to prove or disprove it. Still, it lives on as the simplest of documents, always accessible to the common person and ever more at home in the streets than at the Sorbonne or the ancient halls of Oxford.

Koine! The Vulgate! The Street Book!

God avoided speaking to us in high-toned words meant only to redeem the scholars. Indeed, his words have sometimes confounded the scholars while it redeemed the simple. No wonder Jesus prayed, "I praise you, Father, Lord of heaven and earth, because you have hidden these things from the wise and learned, and revealed them to little children" (Matt. 11:25). The Bible makes little children of all of us. I must confess I never open its pages feeling like a sage or scholar. This is my Father's simple letter to me. I listen as his child. "Jesus love me! This I know" is a child's affirmation for the God of children. I read as a child and he assures me I am his and all I fear or hope for may soon be revealed. I must be childlike or I will miss what I should hear.

It is amazing how university deans and dons can live their lives reading and dissecting the Bible and yet stumble into eternity across the grand simplicities of "Jesus Loves Me." Not so with the children. How easily they catch what the scholars miss! When Martin Luther was asked how he could feel comfortable preaching to the intelligent scholars who thronged his congregation, Luther replied that he did not preach to the scholars, he preached to Hansie and Betsy, two ordinary "housewives" in his congregation. If they understood the Bible's truth, Luther felt, the scholars would have some chance at it.

The issue of faith has always belonged more readily to the simple than the scholarly. The scholars often try too hard. They are more bent on explaining God rather than believing in him. So in the end it is those with a simple, childlike faith who march ahead of them into heaven. They might not have known much of the Bible, but what they did know they believed. Heaven is made more accessible by the quality of our trust than the quantity of our theology.

In the Bible God speaks the vernacular. Why? Because for most of those he loves it is their only language. When Lincoln said that God must have loved the common people because he made so many of them, he perfectly expressed the mind of God. The Bible was too critical to the salvation of all to make it an elitist discussion for the few.

A MESSAGE FROM THE GOD
OF EXIT SIGNS

In some ways the word of God is like the word *Exit* that stands illuminated in dark theaters. Every movie or concert must exist alongside this small, four-letter word. Is it an annoyance to have this brief word shining over the heads of patrons while Pavarotti thrills them with Italian renderings of Verdi's work? No. Why not? Why are all of us so tolerant of this blatant simplicity? Because if the theater should fill with smoke, Pavarotti's aria would dwindle in its excellence while the word *Exit* would take on a special significance. If there is smoke in the concert hall, even Pavarotti will think his aria less important than this word. He too will leave off his lifelong love of the arts and begin looking for a way out.

The *Exit* is there to keep things simple. The sign could say *An Emergency Passage of Egress*. But *Exit* says it more simply and speaks to all. So when God wrote the Bible he kept the message up front and simple. Everybody needs both a way through life and a way out of life. Hence God's Word comes in common Greek, common Latin, common English.

The idea of the importance of biblical simplicity first dawned on me when I was serving in the Philippines. One day while I was reading and meditating on Jesus' powerful words in Matthew 11:5, I realized that one of the evidences of Jesus' messiahship was that the poor have the Good News preached to them. It suddenly occurred to me, as I meditated on the poverty of those Christians among whom I served, that I could see the heart of this passage. Not only were the poor having the gospel preached unto them, but the gospel was about the only good news these poor people would ever get. It is indeed good news that Jesus loves us and the Bible tells us so. How the poor treasure the words of God, for they have no other earthly treasure. The poor of the Philippines had guessed what Woodrow Wilson said so long ago: "A man has deprived himself of the best there is in the world who has deprived himself of this, a knowledge of the Bible."

I have seen old women smiling above their simple, cheap Bibles because they knew they were made rich by its inner treasure. God had something so important to say he dared not write it just for the world's top thinkers.

It was the right way to say it.

The Bible is God's best evidence that he is in love with me. I am among those ordinary persons who are glad to hear it. The *Koine* Greek New Testament can be summarized as simply as "Jesus loves me! This I know, for the Bible tells me so." The Bible—first, last, and always—is a story of Jesus and his love for me.

THE BIBLE: ALIVE AND POWERFUL

The Bible bears witness to its own authentic claims. One of the most insightful passages that deals with its authenticity is Hebrews 4:12: "For the word of God is [alive], and powerful, and sharper than any two edged sword, piercing even to the dividing asunder of soul and spirit, and of the joints and marrow, and is a discerner of the thoughts and intents of the heart" (KJV).

Let us examine what Hebrews 4:12 really means. This text asserts that the Bible is alive and is like a two-edged sword. The word for "sword" used in this passage refers to the Roman infantry swords, the *machaira*. The *machaira* was a short sword that various Roman generals depended on as their vast armies moved out to subdue and create an empire. This eighteen-inch blade was every fighter's confidence.

Many of Rome's enemies carried much longer swords that appeared more frightening in battle. But the short *machaira*, double-edged for cutting both ways, was highly maneuverable in tight battle situations where there was neither the room nor the time to swing longer, less manageable, blades. Many a Gaul, when he saw the "short swords of Rome" coming toward him in battle lines, was prone to be amused— an amusement that shortly ended in what Roman legionnaires thought of as early death syndrome. An entire empire was founded on this short, effective blade.

I am especially in debt to the Bible. It tells me Jesus loves me, but it does ever so much more than this. I see it as God's living Word. It creates and topples empires. It creates its own kingdom from those cruel empires.

I have a dear friend named David who was thrust into Castro's prison after the communists came to power in Cuba. He confessed to me the two things that kept him going until his release nearly four years later. The first of these was his wife, who remained free. She kept their two small boys with her; one of these was just a baby when David was sentenced. Margaret, his wife, each day took the boys and walked past the prison where David could watch her pass. If it was safe, she would linger outside on the sidewalks and play with her sons. Her happy courage became for him a great source of strength.

The other source was his *machaira*. He took the only New Testament to be found in the prison and tore it into segments and passed those portions of the Bible freely among the other Christian inmates. They all read and studied their segments for weeks before passing them on to others. This living Word brought life. This all-powerful *machaira* chopped through the depressing, long years of their confinement.

When Karl Barth began pastoring his war-torn parish at Safenwil during World War I, he confessed he had been schooled on liberal theology that nearly always carries the temptation to doubt the Bible. Barth finally moved in the direction of a more conservative theology because he felt the times were too desperate to preach a doubtful Word. At such a time only the living *Machaira,* the "sword-Word" of God, would do.

The best evidence that the Bible is alive is its overall, day-to-day effectiveness in our own lives. When I read it, my life is changed from defeat to victory. It is a certain victory-based Jesus love. He loves me, this I know. For the Bible says so. The Christ who loves me lives at the center of this book and produces an incredible confidence in the center of my uncertainty.

But the final evidence that this book is the living Word of God is that it deals with the deep-down, secret issues of our lives. The Scriptures! How deeply they reach into our very interiors. I fly to the word to hear it speak in any number of circumstances. When I have quailed in terror before something God expected of me I have quoted Joshua 1:9: "Have not I commanded thee? Be strong and of a good courage; be not afraid, neither be thou dismayed: for the Lord thy God is with thee whithersoever thou goest" (KJV).

When I have felt my financial resources too small to

go on I have heard the apostle Paul shouting to me: "But my God shall supply all your needs according to his riches in glory by Christ Jesus" (Phil. 4:19 KJV).

When I have been bludgeoned into a weariness of soul by the onslaught of too many problems, I have heard the exaltation of Isaiah: "But they that wait upon the LORD shall renew their strength; they shall mount up with wings as eagles; they shall run, and not be weary; and they shall walk, and not faint" (Isa. 40:31 KJV).

When I have lost my path into a foggy future, I have heard the psalmist singing: "Trust in the LORD, and do good; so shalt thou dwell in the land, and verily thou shalt be fed" (Ps. 37:3 KJV).

The Word of God pierces down into the unseeable me to release the invisible God. It floods my uncertain way with life.

Ambrose Bierce incorrectly quipped, "A Christian is one who believes that the New Testament is a divinely inspired book admirably suited to the spiritual needs of his neighbour." I have never found this the case. It is our hearts that are pierced by God's *machaira*—our souls that are purified. The Bible works deep down and its chief work is to remind us that Jesus loves us.

HOW DOES THE BIBLE SPEAK OF JESUS' LOVE?

How can I be sure the child's hymn is right? Does the Bible tell me Jesus loves me? If so, it is the most welcome of news in my largely loveless world.

I can see that Jesus loves me when I examine how he loves the whole world. This theme resonates throughout Scripture. This is the kind of love often expressed through great humanitarians such as David and Holocaust-survivor Corrie ten Boom. To love Jesus is to care about other people. I personally believe that certain missionaries have given selflessly of their money and years because they were in love with the people they served.

The New Testament word for this kind of love is *agape*. It is the most noble of Greek words for "love." It is love for its own sake. *Agape* operates without reference to its subject. It requires no return. God loves with this kind of love. It is love for the unlovely. It serves without recompense.

It is cross love!

Agape is how Jesus loves me. His love for me is completely selfless. The great preacher Elijah Brown said of Jesus:

> Not the slightest evidence of selfishness or self-interest can be found in the story of his life. He was always helping others but not once did he do anything to help himself. He had the power to turn stones into bread but went hungry forty days without doing it . . . His first miracle was performed, not before a multitude to spread his own fame, but in a far away hamlet, to save a peasant's wife from humiliation. He . . . wept over Jerusalem, but he never had any mercy on himself.[1]

"Jesus loves me" is the simplest reduction of such redeeming truth. He loves me in spite of the fact that I can do nothing for him. He loves me because he cannot help himself. I love him because I am helpless without his love.

Jesus' sacrificial death is the highest expression of this love. When you look up *agape* in an English dictionary, there should be a picture of the cross. And maybe the only words of definition would be those old lines of poet Edwin Arlington Robinson: "Stung by the mob that came to see the show, The Master toiled along to Calvary."[2]

HOW CAN WE KNOW HIS LOVE TOWARD US IS CONSTANT?

The Bible informs me that Jesus' love toward me will always be there. Jesus himself, in the last words he ever said on the planet, assured me this was true. "Surely I am with you always, to the very end of the age," he said (Matt. 28:20). All that God said, therefore, of his own Spirit to the psalmist is true of Jesus. The question came: "Where can I go from your Spirit? Where can I flee from your presence?" (Ps. 139:7). The answer is implied: nowhere!

> *If I go up to the heavens, you are there;*
> *If I make my bed in the depths, you are there.*
> *If I rise on the wings of the dawn,*
> *if I settle on the far side of the sea,*
> *even there your hand will guide me,*
> *your right hand will hold me fast.*
> *If I say, "Surely the darkness will hide me*
> *and the light become night around me,"*
> *even the darkness will not be dark to you;*
> *the night will shine like the day,*
> *for darkness is as light to you.* (Ps. 139:8–12)

Jesus is ever present. Indeed, he is omnipresent. There is nowhere we may flee from his presence.

Does the Bible really tell me that his love for me is unfailing? Yes, beyond all doubt. If Psalm 139 is not enough, then consider the words of the apostle Paul on two occasions. First, when he suffered a shipwreck in the Mediterranean he said to the doomed sailors who sailed on the same vessel with him: "Last night an angel of the God whose I am and whom I serve stood beside me and said . . . 'God has graciously given you the lives of all who sail with you. So keep up your courage, men'"(Acts 27:23–25). God was reminding Paul he would not forsake him.

In another passage Paul is facing his trial before Nero. It is a trial from which he was certainly never released—a trial from which he was surely martyred. Even there he said: "At my first defense, no one came to my support, but everyone deserted me. May it not be held against them. But the Lord stood at my side and gave me strength . . . And I was delivered from the lion's mouth. The Lord will rescue me from every evil attack and will bring me safely to his heavenly kingdom" (2 Tim. 4:16–18).

All through his life Paul faced the horrors and rigors of all that God required from him, knowing that God was with him. In 2 Corinthians 3:23–30 he testified to the presence of Christ who stood by him during his sufferings:

I have . . . been in prison more frequently, been flogged more severely, and been exposed to death again and again. Five times I received from the Jews forty lashes minus one. Three times I was beaten with rods, once I was stoned, three times I was shipwrecked, I spent a day and a night in the open sea. I have been constantly on the move. I have been in danger from rivers, in danger from bandits, in danger from my own countrymen, in danger from Gentiles; in danger in the city, in danger in the country, in danger at sea; and in danger from false brothers. I have labored and toiled and often gone without sleep; I have known hunger and thirst and have often gone without food; I have been cold and naked. Besides everything else, I face daily the pressure of my concern for all the churches. Who is weak, and I do not feel weak? Who is led into sin, and I do not inwardly burn?

If I must boast, I will boast of the things that show my weakness.

How do I know that Jesus loves me and that his love is constant? The Bible tells me so. He loves me more than I could ever deserve. He loves me with the stead-fast assurance that he will never leave me. When the chips are down, the banners of heaven are up. When none can be found to take their stand beside me, he is there, constant and unfailing.

CONCLUSION

How do we know who Jesus is and what he did? The Bible tells us. Who trusts what the Bible says of Jesus? Everyone who ever tipped his hat in Jesus' direction. Look at this list of notables and what they said of Jesus:

author and ad executive Bruce Barton called him the greatest salesman who ever lived. Poet T. S. Eliot called him Christ, the Tiger. German theologian Karl Rahner thought of him as a perfect human person. Author J. A. T. Robinson called him the human face of God. German author and theologian Paul Tillich referred to him as the New Being. Theologian Dietrich Bonhoeffer called him the man for others, musical genius Andrew Lloyd Webber a "superstar." Where did all of these ideas come from? From the Bible. It is the ultimate sourcebook on who Jesus is and what he requires.

Such scriptural evidence requires a wonderful response from us. Missionary Amy Carmichael of India sang out her praises for the everlasting, ever-faithful Christ when she wrote: "Love through me, Love of God . . . O love that faileth not, break forth, and flood this world of thine."[3] And she begged the ever-present Christ to use her as a channel through which God might love his entire world: "Pour through me now, I yield myself to thee. Love, blessed love, do as thou wilt with me . . . O the passion of Thy loving, O the Flame of Thy Desire! Melt my heart with thy great loving, set me all aglow, afire!"[4] Then shall we sing of Jesus' love, a love we feel in all the pages of God's Holy Word.

My first encounter with Jesus came when I was nine years old. The evangelist who was preaching told me I needed Jesus as my Savior. If it had been his only line of salesmanship, I would likely never have bought what he was selling. But all the time he talked, he held a Bible in his hand. He assured me that Christ loved me . . . while he waved his Bible in the air. God was in love with me, the evangelist said, and the certification of that love was in the Book. He made a good solid connection. It took. I have never been able to separate Christ's love from that Book. I've never wanted to. "Jesus loves me! This I know, for the Bible tells me so."

QUESTIONS FOR REFLECTION

1. Why do you think that God inspired the Bible to be written in "street Greek" rather than in the language of the scholars?

2. Why do you think that Martin Luther insisted on preaching to Hansie and Betsy rather than the scholars who attended his sermons?

3. Read Hebrews 4:12. What are some ways the Scriptures have helped you hack through the difficulties of your life? Describe one experience in which you felt some particular Bible passage fully met your need.

4. How do the scriptures help you deal with the "secret issues" of your life? In what way have you allowed God's Word to make you open and candid about who God has called you to be and your purpose in the world?

5. In what way do the Scriptures help us build a confidence in God that we are always loved? What does the phrase "The Bible tells me so" really mean to you?

6. Psalms 139 is used here as a picture of the presence of God in our lives. In what ways does the passage certify that we can know God will never forsake us?

7. Consider what the Apostle Paul said in 2 Corinthians 11:23–30. Is God actually with us in the kind of trials

set forth in this passage? How can we learn some form of Bible study that will make this kind of confidence ever dependable in our lives?

8. What did Amy Carmichael mean when she said, "love through me, Love of God"? Is that a reasonable prayer for all of us? How can the Bible teach us this kind of disciplined loving?

CHAPTER 6

Little Ones to Him Belong

"Are you going to do a miracle today?"

Wherever Jesus went, children seemed to follow. They wanted to see him heal a cripple or zap a fig tree, to say hello to him, to tell him something special.

"Don't shoo them away!" said Jesus to his friends.

"But you don't have time for this foolishness," said Judas.

"I've got the time."

"You don't have enough time to sleep. You don't have enough time to pray. You don't have enough time to spend with your friends," said Judas. "So how come you've enough time to spend with these noisy, runny-nosed children?"

"Because they're so much fun," said Jesus.

The boys and girls crowded around the great man. Jesus asked who they were, did they pray for their mothers and fathers, was Solomon a judge or a prophet or a king, weren't Ruth and Miriam and Deborah the real heroes of the Scriptures, and no, he wasn't going to do any tricks today.

"Heaven is a lot like a playground," Jesus said to Judas later, "and unless you remember what it was like to be a child, you won't get in."

"Does that mean I have to hop, skip and jump forever?" asked Judas.

"No," said Jesus. "It means you have to be curious and eager and good and honest and fair."

WILLIAM GRIFFIN[1]

A CONVERSATION WITH JESUS

Sometimes I find children a bit noisy and offensive, don't you?

Never! Children are but replicas of all that heaven is about. Offensive they could never be till angels hate their hallelujahs and the seraphim consider praise a waste of time. Children are images of trust, so allow all little children to come unto me— for such is the Kingdom of heaven.

But the path of greatness requires mature thinking and action, doesn't it?

Hardly. The path of greatness lies in the bending of our knees and not in our stiff intention to climb to greatness. All who are noble of character must kneel and wait till God touches them upon the shoulder with the sword of servanthood. Whoever humbles himself like a little child, is greatest in the kingdom of heaven.

But worship requires an adult mentality, doesn't it? Remember on Palm Sunday when the children began to shout, "Hosanna to the Son of David." Remember what an uproar they caused. Remember how disruptive they were?

Can honest praise disrupt the King of heaven?

Noisy children could never make my Father angry. Rather it is the cacophony of adult hypocrisy that drowns out all celestial praise. Have you never read, "From the lips of children and infants God has ordained praise"?

What is heaven's view of child abuse?

If a child asks for an egg, would a good father ever give him a scorpion? If he asks for a fish, would a loving father give him a snake? The best fathers know how to give good gifts. As for abusive fathers, it would be better if a millstone were tied about their neck and they were drowned in the depths of the sea.

Don't hold back, Jesus, tell us how you really feel.

Whoever welcomes a little child in my name welcomes me. My Father is not willing to lose a single one of these. Heaven sends the warrior angels, with fiery swords aloft. They fly around the great abyss of time to make certain that no child is lost. Children throng the corridors of heaven making innocence a virtue of eternity.

MATTHEW 19:14; 18:4; 21:16; MARK 10:16;
MATTHEW 7:9–11; 18:5, 6, 10, 14

From birth to new-birth we are all members of God's family. Near the beginning of Jesus' ministry, his mother and brothers came to take him back home to Nazareth. They seemed embarrassed that Jesus, Mary's son and their sibling, was going about preaching that he was the Son of God. His family needed his instruction so Jesus firmly spoke his mind. His family would no longer be defined as those who shared his bloodline. Now his family would include all those who were willing to call his Father their father.

The line "Little ones to Him belong" makes it clear that children are welcome in Christianity.

I came to Christ as a boy, but even then I was struck by the notion that God was my Father and Christ, therefore, was my Brother. In the little church where I came to faith, the members called each other Brother and Sister and so my need to be included in the family of God was well met. Families (when not dysfunctional) are wonderful places where need and love come in balance. All our lives they remain the best habitat for making life work.

It was Anselm who spoke of the Trinity by saying that God is within himself "a sweet society." The Scriptures always speak of God in the masculine, but lest we blow God's masculinity out of proportion, let us be honest enough to say that the Scriptures abound with powerful feminine symbols of God as well. The Bible does not lead us to call God our Mother, as some theologians insist. But all good theologians know that the Scriptures teem with images of motherhood that relate to our faith. And where these exist, they often speak of God as the nourisher.

GOD'S NOURISHMENT OF HIS LITTLE ONES

The psalmist may have offered us the fullest insight into the nourishing aspects of God when he cried, "I will lift up mine eyes unto the hills, from whence cometh my help" (Ps. 121:1 KJV). The word translated as "hill" here is the Hebrew word *shad*. *Shad* is also the word for "breast." This word is used in combination with the Hebrew word for God, *El*, in the word *El-Shaddai*. Why? Why would Hebrews use the same word for "hill" or "breast" that they use for God? If we concede that hills are breast-shaped and freely confess that it is to the breast we first go in life for nourishment, *El-Shaddai* becomes the God of the hills, the God of the breast . . . the God who nourishes.

As appetites go, we are born hungry. We must eat or die.

Jesus speaks to me most eloquently when he refers to himself as the "bread come down from heaven" (see John 6:33). He pointed to himself as our soul's nourishment. How often, when I am starved for sustenance, when my spirit is malnourished and my soul famished, have I gone to him and found strength? Jesus alone nourishes me when every other source of strength fails me.

"Little ones to Him belong" reminds us that God is the model Parent. There is little doubt that parents will go a long way to meet their children's needs. I remember as a child that when Mother packed our lunches—later to be opened and observed by our class-mates—she took far more care with our lunch than hers. I got the good, firm apples while she took the softer ones. I got the best bread on my sandwiches while she took the older, staler slices.

The whole world was recently touched by the story of a Slavic woman who was victimized by an earthquake. She was trapped under tons of concrete with her little daughter. After her eventual rescue, she revealed a compelling tale. Her daughter had whimpered during their terrifying ordeal because she was thirsty. The mother, who could barely move one arm, cut herself with a piece of glass. The child literally drank her blood and lived. If the illustration seems gory, remember it actually happened. But more than that it remains a great example that a loving parent will go to almost any length to nourish her child.

"Little ones to Him belong" means that God sees me as his child. He ever nourishes me in my weakness. Like any needy child I go to him in my hunger. He scoops me up in his everlasting arms, and his bread is ever abundant. I eat. I live! Because of grace I know his filling. I have an insatiable appetite for the bread that only heaven can supply. That bread is Jesus.

THE POTENTIAL OF GOD'S LITTLE ONES

The adult world is an orb of power and control. But the power-mongers really do very little for God. There is little potential of godliness in these couriers of commerce. Children, on the other hand, are all potential. Their ever-stretching future is their finest asset. Think of all that baby Werner von Braun or baby William Shakespeare once represented. During their infancies the world ruled that these babies were normal and needy. Their parents fed them, making possible a seven-pound literary giant or a six-pound nuclear physicist. These babies ate and grew. They owned the future but rarely saw their greatness.

Babies are perfect pictures of trust. Picked up and passed around a clumsy circle of adults, they never recoil in fear or stop to ponder whether they might be dropped. Especially where their parents are concerned, children show that trust is as natural to them as belonging. It is only with adulthood they see how foolish they have been. Then suddenly they know that trust is folly. But the doubt they arrive at is not totally useless. Willful doubt is how we keep the world from hurting us.

The most notable quality of babies is their dependency on others. They cannot move unless others carry them. They will die of thirst unless someone brings them water. They will die of hunger unless someone gives them food. Adults are moved by their pitiable, helpless crying to relieve their pain and nourish their hunger.

God is endeared to us when in our helplessness we turn and cry for his supply. The current status of children in the world owes much to Jesus. Each time I pass a billboard that reads, "Never hurt a child. Never, never!" I know there is direct relationship between the existence of that billboard and the centuries-long influence of Christ.

Jesus clearly expressed his love for children when he

decided to become one. Alphonsus de Liguori pointed this out:

> When the Son of God became man for our sake, He could have come on earth as an adult man from the first moment of his human existence. But since the sight of little children draws us with an especial attraction to love them, Jesus chose to make his first appearance on earth as a little infant . . . "God wished to be born as a little baby," wrote Saint Peter Chrysologus, "in order that He might teach us to love and not to fear him." The prophet Isaiah had long before foretold that the Son of God was to be born as an infant and thus give himself to us on account of the love he bore us: "A child is born to us, a son is given to us."[2]

There is immense potential in children.

At the nexus where children's potential meets their helplessness stands parenthood. The parent takes infantile helplessness and teaches it self-reliance. Then at last childish helplessness begins to develop the confidence to bring God-given gifts to fruition.

LITTLE ONES TO HIM BELONG: FAITH SHALL BRING JOY

A child's joy is often too wild to be tamed by parental management. My daughter Melanie taught me this in 1968. She was seven years old and for Christmas that year I had bought her a cheap little Kodak "Brownie" camera. That same Christmas I got a rather sophisticated 35mm camera, replete with dials, gauges, and meters. We both opened our cameras on Christmas morning and as our various yuletide visitors stopped by to give us the regards of the day we took them out, backed our guests up to the Christmas tree, and said "Smile." At that moment Melanie took their picture. But I was insecure. My camera required more understanding. This was a long ago day when cameras were not so automatic as they have since become. So before I could snap a single picture I always needed to check and set the f-stop mechanism. So I said "Smile" while I performed this function. Then I said "Smile" again. They did, but now I had to stop and check the "foot distance to subject dial." If all was well, I said "Smile" yet again. Then I glanced at the light meter to be sure the setting was right. Then after I said "Smile" one final time, I took their picture.

Melanie and I took a lot of pictures that Christmas season and when it was over I took both rolls of film—hers and mine—to the developer. Two weeks later I went back to pick them up. It was very difficult for me to tell which set of pictures I liked the best—hers or mine. Oh, mine were much clearer than hers, but the people in her pictures looked truly happy, while mine looked like they had been smiling for a while.

Children have a natural and spontaneous joy in the presence of Jesus. Remember in Matthew's account of Palm Sunday, it is the children who seem to be laughing and shouting their hosannas. How often we should let them teach us their praise and certainly their laughter. Joy often erupts from exuberant children as an effervescent mixture of praise and laughter.

LITTLE ONES TO HIM BELONG: GOD'S GRACE WELCOMES HIS LITTLE ONES

I will forever remember the time when, as a little one myself, I came to Christ. I was sitting spellbound in a prairie tent revival. I remember first being drawn to the tent as I watched those who put it up. I thought it was a circus tent and that Ringling Brothers was coming to our small town. But then I watched as the workers put up a big sign that said REVIVAL. I was so disappointed. In those days I agreed with Tom Sawyer, who said, "Church ain't shucks to a circus."

But I could not stay disappointed long.

I must confess I made no immediate plans to attend the circus that had "degenerated" into a revival. But then a neighborhood chum of mine was forced by his parents to attend that revival (that we both had hoped might be a circus). My little friend was not a model child. Even the brattiest of children would have called him a brat. But when he went to the revival he came home "saved"!

"Saved?" I asked. "Who saved you?"

"Jesus!" he exulted.

"Why would Jesus save you when your folks have been trying to drown you for nine years?" I asked. I was utterly bewildered by the things he was telling me.

"You must come with me tonight to the big tent," he said.

And so I did.

The memory of it is with me yet. The huge tent was a canvas cathedral perfumed by the smell of fresh sawdust that had been scattered around to provide a soft and aromatic floor. Benches had been constructed out of concrete blocks and wood planks. There were two large men who played accordions and sang gospel tunes. Fireflies danced hypnotically around the light-bulbs. It was all exotic and thrilling.

The handsome young preacher wore a buckskin jacket decorated with leather fringe. His wide gestures painted graphic pictures of hell, causing the willowy leather thongs of his jacket to swing and swirl, mes-merizing me. His words flew at me. I could not resist their penetration into my heart.

Yet standing at the center of this wonderful evening was Jesus. Jesus was not complicated. He was the friend of children. The evangelist who professed to know him very well said that Jesus was especially fond of children. The more he painted his portrait of Jesus, the more I was astonished that Christ was so simple to understand. I flew to Jesus. It was easy. Any child could get saved and sanctified, he said, by feeling bad about his sins and calling Jesus "Lord." Feeling bad about my sins was both easy and honest for me. It was my duty. After all, the evangelist said, it was my iniquities that had "nailed Jesus to the cross." Odd, but I never felt his words too severe.

At that age I never thought of comparing my sins with those of Al Capone. Still, they seemed black enough to me and so I hurried to the mourner's bench and confessed them. I was washed in the blood of the Lamb. Sure enough, the evangelist was right! Jesus became my special friend. He has been ever since.

THE ABBA GOD OF THE LITTLE ONES

"Papa" is often the first word a child says, and gloriously it is a word of relationship. If the two-syllable utterance brings such joy to human parents, should we be surprised to see the joy it brings to our divine Parent?

What a sweet symphony Jesus brought the race when he came calling God "Father." How often we resort to this strong word. Actually, Jesus used the term *Abba,* a word not so akin to *Father* as to *Papa,* a word we usually learn before we learn the word *Father.* We come to own this word when we are tiny, needy, and dependent. So the word still lives in my sixty-four-year-old heart. I still find it easy to think of God as Papa.

Further, the word *Abba* connotes *Abbot*—a priest, a surrogate father for the spiritual orphans of the world. My suspicion is that most of us never really have all the fathering we want in life. Our earthly fathers may have done their job well, and most have done the best they could. Still we feel the need for more fatherhood.

I believe this need causes many pastors to become a kind of father figure to their churches. As a young pastor I would often feel I filled this need for men even older than I was. These men needed counsel, prayer, understanding, guidance. All of these are things earthly fathers can supply. So it is not difficult to see why the word *Father* came to be applied to clergymen.

As a child I treasured the fatherhood of God. My father abandoned my mother with his nine children, and though she raised us with maximum love and input, still I believe what I wanted and most needed as a child was a father.

It would be years before I came to manhood. I then went to seminary to study the life of Christ and learn more about the Nazarene who had so changed my life. There at last I began to see that the Man of Galilee was more complex than I—as a child—was led to believe.

But the key thing was that I didn't have to unlearn anything to continue on into a more adult study of

Jesus. What I learned that night in the tent has stood unchanged by all the later scholarship I would someday encounter. This all proves that Jesus forever makes himself accessible to his children by keeping things simple.

Let us further examine what we have already affirmed. Christ's love of his children and his desire to be accessible to them should never be called into question. It is his great Fatherlike love that elicits the love of his children. The Abba God is the Daddy God that elicits all that is deepest and most emotive within us. His love for us, his special little ones, whether we are seven or seventy, calls forth our responsive love for him.

Once, while I was serving a church in Omaha and teaching at the seminary in Kansas City, my professional responsibilities required me to fly every week to Kansas City. My first-grade son noticed I was gone all the time. He had no idea where I was going nor what I was doing there. I sensed a chasm growing between us. He became more and more remote. Finally, I began to understand the reason: he felt there was some exotic part of his daddy's life he didn't know. When I sensed that he was slipping away from me emotionally, I said to him, "Son, would you like to fly on the plane with me to Kansas City to see where Daddy works?"

His eyes brightened. It was great to see them light up. They hadn't in a while.

So I arranged to get him a ticket and on the appointed day we flew off. When we arrived on campus I had much to do. He sat quietly at the back of classes I taught. Wherever I went on the campus, he tagged along after me. He met all my friends and came to know a part of my life he had never seen before.

With that trip a wonderful and new thing began to occupy us. We were one again. Our relationship grew close. My Abba status had been restored. He had come to know everything about me that could be known and I was his Papa again.

In some such way, Jesus understood our need to know our heavenly Father. Bit by bit, he showed us the nature of Abba God, even the hidden things of God that we thought might be forever inaccessible to us. We learned from Jesus that God is love, that he cares about all his children. We learned that it was never God's intention that any child should ever live or die without knowing him.

HOMESICKNESS: THE GRAND LONGING

We spend the first third of our lives trying to figure out how to get away from home and the last two-thirds trying to figure out how to get back. This homesickness is marked by the very powerful allurements we cannot live without, the first of which is love. However far we travel from home, we cannot escape the feeling that somewhere back near the beginning of our lives, we were loved. We were loved unconditionally whether we were good or bad, horrid or deserving. But the farther we move from those protected years, the more we discover the world is indifferent to us. It doesn't hate or love us, it merely coexists with us in a blasé fashion.

Even as older adults we remember our childhood years as a time when love was as predictable as sunrise. My family recently celebrated the one-hundredth anniversary of my mother's birth. She passed away some years ago, but a powerful urge drew all seven of us remaining siblings together. We, her living children, are all in our sixties to eighties, but we gathered together to talk of her life. It was both beautiful and haunting to hear us "older folks" sit and talk vibrantly of the love we once found in her presence. What was the significance of our gathering? We had come together to affirm the first value of homesickness: love!

The second value of this grand longing was a sense that our home life was safe. I well remember my mother's anger when a group of high school bullies (I was in junior high at the time) caught me, hauled me from my bicycle, and beat me up. I can remember crying my way home from the experience. And I will never forget my mother's instant hostility toward those bullies. Somehow I had known, that very night, that if I could get home, I would be was safe. There life was protected.

I can remember as a child being afraid of the dark, as many children are. I was afraid of those dark imaginary demons and fiends who terrorize trembling children at night. On those nights I played late at a friend's house, I knew if I could get home—where Mother was—I would be safe. There were no monsters big enough to intimidate the Miller children in the presence of their fearless mother.

But the one final symbol, the third value of homesickness, is abundance. My mother had most of her children before the Depression dawned. As I look back now, I know life in these days had to be hard, but Mother created from her meager living a grand sense of abundance. It is the standard by which I still measure life. Her pies made Marie Callender's look bashful and afraid of fruit. Her biscuits were unexcelled (except, of course, by those my wife bakes). Family reunions were festivals of heaping tables, lemonade, potato salad, plum pies, and lard-fried chicken. (Cholesterol was an unknown word that waited for later generations who would hanker after sunflower seeds and lettuce leaves.) I know now that during the depression we lived close to the edge, yet my mother created such a sense of abundance that it seemed to us we never lacked for anything.

In my childish mind, home was abundance. I can see why Jesus lured the poor disciples of century one by telling them he had come to give them "abundant life." No wonder heaven holds such allurement to the Christian. In heaven the words "doing without" do not exist. Need has never been permitted in the presence of God. No wonder author Peter Kreeft said heaven is the heart's deepest longing. We want to go home now—forever. We are homesick.

But homesickness is a disease of childhood. And it's terminal, I'm afraid. I can understand why psychologist Abraham Maslow said most of us never leave adolescence. Why? Because adolescence is our favorite time of reflecting on home. Adolescence is where children spend half their childhoods. It is sometimes a monstrous and hideous age that tries the foundations of love. Our parents are torn between helping us get out of the home and trying to figure out how to make birth control retroactive. But for the most part, love wins out.

So adolescence becomes the porch of our entry into a less forgiving world. We enter it and grow old, in some cases leaving our homes far behind. But the longing lives. In our hearts we are forever children, wondering what Daddy would do, what Mama would say. We are children, and the grand respite of our childhood is God. He is Father. We may appear to be adults, even executives to those who don't know us, but to God we are children always in need of help and strength.

We are his children. Love, protection, and abundance will always exist. Home lives! We're headed there! And yet in the love of Christ we live there—we are the little ones who belong to him.

CONCLUSION

Children give their parents the gift of trust.

At just the sound of her father's beckoning voice a child will leap into the darkness of a cellar unable to see a thing. Watch her! There is no hesitation in her leap. Her father has spoken. The mellow tone of his voice is certification beyond what she can see or fear. She leaps because she trusts completely. But she trusts completely because in a thousand previous experiences she has found her father faithful. Since he has never let her down, she is convinced he never will.

It is God's faithfulness that Jesus wants all of us to count on. Yet adults have lived too long in a devious world to find trust easy. Trust is a habit they gave up as they left childhood. They have trusted business alliances, friends, used-car salesmen, and politicians, and all of them have in turn failed. Now at last they come to God, and find the stakes infinitely higher. The Bible says that unless they believe they cannot have eternal life, but they are reluctant to trust God. They are reluctant to give him more than they have given others. They are afraid of committing themselves.

It was into such a ring of doubt that Jesus sat a child and said, "Unless you become like little children you will never enter the kingdom of heaven" (Matt. 18:2). Remember, this happened when the disciples were pondering the question of who would be greatest in God's kingdom. Ambition was the disciples' preoccupation. They wanted to be first in the kingdom. The children Jesus loved were not driven by any such need for power.

In each of us our ambitious drives must reckon with what God requires trust: abundant and eternal. Children believe what they are told. If we tell them there is a Santa Claus they will believe it. It may not speak much for their discretion. It nearly always reveals some naïveté. But they do believe.

They are convinced partly by their parents' love for them. Though they could never articulate it, they know they are loved by a love too sincere to betray them.

Augustine of Hippo wrote in beautiful language of the child's, be he seven or seventy—relentless longing for the God who is his true Home and Parent: "O beauty so ancient and so new . . . You called, you cried, you shattered my deafness. You sparkled, you blazed, you drove away my blindness. You shed your fragrance, and I drew in my breath, and I pant for you. I tasted and now I hunger and thirst. You touched me, and now I burn with longing for your peace."[3]

This love breeds its own addiction. It is the same passion that redeems us. It is child's play. It is duck soup. Jesus has accomplished it all and we are his evermore. We gain his presence forever by learning a child's love for his Father, by learning to call God "Abba." We have gained our position in God not in the process of becoming mature thinkers but in the very act of trusting what we could never think through. We are the little ones who belong to him. He is the basis of our hope.

QUESTIONS FOR REFLECTION

1. Several statements are made in the beginning of the chapter as to how far human parents will go to be sure their children are nurtured. How have you felt God's leadership and care in this kind of personal, inner, spiritual nourishment of your own life?

2. As in the author's story of his trip to Kansas with his son, do you think it is true that what children want most from their parents is presence? Why or why not? What are some ways that you crave Christ's presence in your life?

3. Why does this chapter assert that abundance is the final symbol of home?

4. Several have spoken of our desire for heaven as "homesickness." What does this metaphor mean to you? Have you ever been homesick for earthly places and people? Have you ever felt that strongly in regard to heaven? Do you think that people can ever be as homesick for heaven as they are for someplace on this earth without being terminally ill or in great pain? Explain why you feel the way you do.

5. Much is made in this chapter of a child's leap of faith. Have you ever leapt at the mere command of God when he wanted you to do something impossible? How did it work out? Would you have the courage to do the same thing again?

CHAPTER 7

They Are Weak, but He Is Strong

We rest on Thee, our Shield and Defender,
We go not forth alone against the foe.
Strong in Thy Strength, safe in Thy keeping
   tender,
We rest on Thee, and in Thy name we go.

Yea, in Thy name, O Captain of Salvation,
In Thy blest name, all other names above,
Jesus our Righteousness, our sure Foundation,
Our Prince of Glory, and our King of Love.

We go in faith, our own great weakness feeling,
And needing more each day Thy grace to know,
Yet from our hearts a song of triumph pealing,
We rest on Thee, and in Thy name we go.

We rest on Thee, our Shield and Defender,
Thine is the battle, Thine shall be the praise.
When passing through the gates of pearly
   spendor,
Victors, we rest with Thee through endless days.

SOURCE UNKNOWN

A CONVERSATION WITH JESUS

Jesus, I feel so often that my world is bigger than I am, that my circumstances are too tangled for my weakness to unravel.

Blessed are you when you face the end of your capabilities—when you can see that your own strength to climb is smaller than the mountain you face. The beginning of every successful conquest is knowing where you are not able. Your strength does have its limits. Mine does not. Take heart, I have triumphed over the world.

But my problems seem to have no solution. They seem impossible.

Your purse alone cannot purchase the solution. But God shall supply all your needs from his riches in glory. With God everything is possible.

But how can I appropriate this great possibility, for in myself I am so weak?

Whatsoever you ask for in prayer, believing, you shall receive. Prayer that flies to heaven unencumbered by the weight of doubt sets free the winds of God's probability.

But can I apply your strength to all my problems?

Trust me! Your doubts seem large only because

you're so small. Seen against the towering might of heaven, they are small indeed. So trust in the Lord and do good; then you shall dwell safely in the land and you shall be fed.

But can I defeat all my circumstances simply by clothing myself with your power?

Satan is but weakness serving evil. He knows he can terrify you but he has never faced God with self-confidence. He cannot make you afraid if you stand with God. Indeed, I saw Satan himself fall from heaven like lightning. Know that I have given you power to trample on the most deadly enemies of man and to overcome all of Satan's might. Nothing will harm you.

Can I depend on you to help me in every moment of weakness, for as long as I live?

I will never leave you nor forsake you. I am with you all the way, even to the end of the world. Dismiss the weakness you fear. Trust. My grace is sufficient for you. My strength is made perfect in weakness.

JOHN 16:33; PHILIPPIANS 4:19; MATTHEW 19:26;
MARK 11:24; PSALM 37:3; LUKE 10:18–19; HEBREWS 13:5;
MATTHEW 28:20; 2 CORINTHIANS 12:9

Abraham Kidunaia lived in the sixth century. His parents were overbearingly secular. They dismissed his insistence that he was called to be a priest and attempted to force him into an arranged marriage. Frustrated by his need to be obedient unto God, Abraham fled into the desert to escape his parents' control and from that point on learned to reckon with hunger and poverty. To keep himself alive he carried a bowl from place to place, begging people to fill it with any kind of food. But he was not just begging from people. He begged, as he saw it, from God alone, who always supplied his need with strength.

I have devoted a part of my life to studying holy men and women of old, but Abraham Kidunaia captures my heart in offering me his fine symbol—an empty bowl. He lifted his bowl to God and begged its filling. I want to find myself daily at the dispensary of heaven, begging God to meet my own needs. Then after I lift my needs to God, I want to trust him to supply them. Had he known the hymn, Kidunaia would have made this his life anthem: "Fill my cup, Lord, I lift it up, Lord, come and ease this hunger in my soul."[1] Our symbol is a bowl. God's definition of our need is a trust in his abundance.

"We are weak, but He is strong."

Helplessness is a common emotion. I had not traveled very far down the highway of faith before I began to feel I was too small to carry all the weight that life sometimes placed on me. In my thirty-five years as a pastor, I often wept and prayed with people who felt they were smaller than their problems.

In time I came to see that there was one great, first step in handling my problems. I had to admit that I was too small to carry them on my own. God can never really help those who feel they are adequate to handle their problems. Self-sufficiency isolates our need from God's supply. Better we should approach God with empty bowls, begging him to fill our insufficiency. "We are weak, but He is strong."

SELF-SUFFICIENCY: THE OBSTRUCTION TO GOD'S ABUNDANCE

Abraham Kidunaia understood this one great truth: whatever we love more than God is god to us. But there are not a lot of categories of things we love that stand opposite to God. Generally our worst idolatries are lavished on ourselves. The man who worships his automobile more than God is really only worshiping his own ego. The only way he can esteem himself is by imagining himself in relation to his car. The student who wins the school competition to be elected to the cheerleading team may only be serving the low, low altar of her popularity.

The gods of our indulgence are many. One of these gods is sexual narcissism. This is the day of the body-god. This god is lord of the abs, pecs, and muscle-building gadgets. Of all the forms of self-love this dress-down god is among the oldest of our goggle-eyed idolatries. The "last-chance" racks at supermarket checkout stands feature a bevy of nearly naked Aphrodites smiling up from slick magazines. Underneath their photos are the allurements: "I dropped a dress size in a single weekend," "I drank Belly-Go and lost 50 pounds in 60 days," or "I'm lighter, I'm lovelier, I'm me!"

Beside these thinning Aphrodites are an equal number of chesty Adonises, strutting from slick tabloids named *Men's Hygiene, Muscles, Macho and Meaty.* These Adonises are braggart hunks whose methodologies promise to transform the pudgy-and-pimply hopefuls clustered at the magazine racks from Buddha to Zeus.

This body adoration in Christian churches takes the most unusual of forms. I once heard of a book called *I Prayed Myself Slim.* The book was the testimony of a twenty-year-old "waddling walrus" who got Jesus on her side and lost eighty-three pounds. God be praised! Jesus had seen to it that her cellulite had been replaced with firm flesh and she was now enjoying date after date, and she was giving all glory to God that she was 38-24-38.

There are many church and denominational programs to help overweight believers become underweight testimonies to the power of prayer. How is it done? Sing hymns and count those fat grams. If you want to speed the work along, you can always join the church's "Work Out for Jesus Club" where you can do aerobics to contemporary Christian music and worship while you work it off. At last, *Hubba-Hubba* and *Hallelujah* are perfectly met.

But who is really worshiped in all of this? For all the rhetoric about God, the center of all this body adoration still remains the ego. There are plenty of reasons to be healthy, but there are no scriptural injunctions commanding us to look like Hercules. There are commandments to stay healthy, not to be beautiful.

But if a physical workout is demanding, the spiritual disciplines of prayer and ministry are more so. The worship of God has always required much of mere mortals. You cannot win God's esteem on the relatively easy machines of health clubs. To do this, you must bend the knee and confess your need. Then, when your confession meets his strength, you will sing a genuine hallelujah to grace. Your empty bowl is your key to his supply.

CONFESSION: THE ART OF NEEDY TOGETHERNESS

One of my favorite Broadway offerings is a play called *Steel Magnolias*. In this wonderful play, some ordinary small-town pals find that in the debilitating pain of life, they need each other. As the chitchat comes and goes in the beauty parlor where they meet and work, they find healing in their togetherness. Together they can handle death, illness, and divorce, any one of which must get all of them to surrender before it can get any one of them to cry "uncle." As James advises us to do, they, in their own way, confess their faults to one another and pray for one another that they might be healed (James 5:16).

Confession is the basis of all valid relationships.

In fact, confession is the key to strength of character. I have yet to meet the first great person of character who harbored doubt or hid within the soul deep, dark, destructive secrets. I once knew a woman who went to a psychiatrist. She was a depressed and shattered soul whose husband was a sexual addict. Fed by pornography and a traveling salesman's penchant for picking up "tricks" in the cabaret districts of those cities where he worked, he lived an indulgent life that had at last destroyed the heart of their marriage. Yet, for all of her years of suffering, this woman had never once confronted her husband with his addiction. The psychiatrist finally asked the woman, "You mean you and your husband have never really talked about this?"

"No," she said, bursting into tears.

"Why?" insisted the doctor.

"We just didn't," she said.

She had lived a life of untold pain because she was harboring unconfessed hurt and had never found the courage to confront her husband openly. It is not until we confess our sin that we begin to arrive at strength of character.

"I am weak, but He is strong" are words that I recite to God to affirm my weakness and celebrate his strength. These words carry the assumption that I can let his strength replace my weaknesses. Yet I do not know of any way to make that happen without the art of confession. In fact, by trial and painful error I have learned that my confession must become my mode of appropriating his strength.

Coming clean in God's presence is the only hope I have of living clean before him.

Dr. James Dobson was one of the last people to visit with the serial killer Ted Bundy. Bundy, of his own confession, had come from a "fine, Christian home." He had, however, begun to experience the evils of pornography as a child. Listen to Bundy's words taken from his final interview with James Dobson:

I hope no one will try to take the easy way out and blame or otherwise accuse my family of contributing to this because I know, and I'm trying to tell you as honestly as I know how, what happened. I think this is the message I want to get across. As a young boy of 12 or 13, I encountered outside the home . . . in the local grocery store and the local drug stores the soft-core pornography. As young boys do, we explored the backroads and side ways and by-ways of our neighborhood, and often times people would dump garbage and whatever they were cleaning out of the house. From time to time we'd come across pornographic books of a harder nature . . . more graphic you might say, [of] a more explicit nature. . . . I want to emphasize as the most damaging kinds of pornography. Again, I'm talking from personal experience—hard, real, personal experience. The most damaging kinds of pornography are those that involve violence and sexual violence. Because the wedding of those two forces, as I know only too well, brings about behavior that is just too terrible to describe. . . . It happened in stages, gradually. It doesn't necessarily, not to me at least, happen overnight. My experience with pornography that deals on a violent level with sexuality is that once you become addicted to it—and I look at this as a kind of addiction—I would keep looking for more potent, more explicit, more graphic kinds of materials. Until you reach the point where the pornography only goes so far. You reach that jumping-off point where you begin to wonder if maybe actually doing it will give you that which is beyond just reading about it or looking at it.[2]

There rides within Bundy's final words the dying of a closed man who harbored dark secrets. He found no confessional outlet for the evil within him. But inner darkness festers under secret pressure. In time his unconfessed inwardness erupted as open evil.

I am a lover of trees, particularly redwoods. It's not just that they are tall and old as Moses. It's that they remain a fine botanical example of how to stand in the storms of life. Near Santa Cruz, California, are the Henry Cowell Redwoods. They, like all the Pacific Coast redwoods, can tower nearly forty stories above the forest floor. They have stood for centuries because they exemplify the simple truth of James 5:16: there is strength in their needy togetherness. These huge trees have no taproot, a dangerous design flaw for trees that grow so tall. But if you cut any one of them down, a wonderful phenomenon occurs. In a flawless circle around the titan stump will spring up a new fifty-foot circle of redwood saplings, each determined to replace his amputated sister. With such a wonderful botanic commitment, each new tree sets out on its lifelong career towering majesty.

How do these trees survive without a deep root system? Their little roots thrust outward and laterally entwine around the roots of the others in the ring. Once their roots have grown together they are bonded, they can stand. They "hold hands" under the ground. Here's to the redwoods, the mascots of Christian interdependency! We need each other. We must reach out and hold each other up in the storms of life.

FACING OUR WEAKNESS

It often takes a crisis to remind me of just how weak I am.

When I was a young minister, our daughter was born, healthy and strong in every way. I was proud to the point of arrogance. Of course, it is right to be proud in the best sense of the word. But what had I really done to make her beautiful and healthy? Nothing. A healthy child is always the gift of God.

When my son was born, the first year of his life was touch and go. When he was very sick, my pride was swallowed up in an abiding prayer for all I desired for him. I was weak. I could do nothing to make him well. I had to trust in the strength of God to fill my weakness—and my son's—with his sufficiency. Ultimately he became strong and thrived, but during those needy days, I discovered a glorious terror in my weakness.

Every terror is worth the fright it inspires. For terrors remind us of our weaknesses. The apostle said that as we remember our weakness, we dress ourselves in power. Jesus in speaking to Paul said, "My grace is sufficient for you, for my power is made perfect in weakness." Paul responded, "Therefore I will boast all the more gladly about my weaknesses, so that Christ's power may rest on me" (2 Cor. 12:9). This became a liberating philosophy for me. I ought to brag about the things I can't handle instead of the things I can. Bragging of my weaknesses allows me to approach God, holding up my empty bowl. Then I find I can appropriate his strength.

So, properly understood, God allows crisis to create and develop my dependency on him. He allows my crisis to mold me into a creature of strength. Angela Morgan wrote:

When God wants to drill a man . . .
Watch His methods, watch His ways.

How He ruthlessly perfects
Whom He royally elects!
How He hammers him and hurts him,
And with mighty blows converts him.
Into trial shapes of clay which
Only God understands;
While his tortured heart is crying
And he lifts beseeching hands![3]

Thus God makes me strong by letting me undergo the anvil. First the mortar, then the pestle. First I know the heavy crush and then the bright pain. First my weakness, then my bruising, then finally my character.

Hercules was the Roman god thought to furnish the pagans with a strength more than their own. Myth has it that when he was a baby, the jealous gods sent a swarm of serpents into his cradle to kill him. But even as a baby Hercules was not intimidated by snakes. He strangled all the serpents sent to undo him.

Which of us has not felt overwhelmed by the serpents of life? They throng us, writhing and hissing. We quail in terror. Why? We are children and children do not deal well with cobras. We have no ability to strangle serpents on our own. Snake-strangling is beyond us. We seek a surer solution. Yet oddly we are saved by a serpent—a snake of metaphor, a serpent on a pole. As Moses lifted up the serpent in the wilderness, we too lift up the Christ (John 3:14). Then all the woes we thought would destroy us are fully dealt with in the power of the cross. The serpents die. Jesus lives. "We are weak, but He is strong."

I think my early fascination with Christian hymns

came when I was victimized by need. These hymns filled me with the strength of a big God at these times when I didn't feel big. I remember them to this day. There is often one of them lilting through my heart, helping me cope with the world as I come to see it and know it. Think of each of these old hymns and the promises they offer:

- O safe to the Rock that is higher than I
- He hideth my soul in the cleft of the rock
- I am weak, but Thou art strong; Jesus, keep me from all wrong
- Oh, Jesus is a Rock in a weary land
- How firm a foundation, ye saints of the Lord
- How great Thou art
- Rock of Ages, cleft for me

How much I depend upon his strength for my support when life gets bigger than I am. There is an old African-American hymn that says it best for me: "The very time I thought that I was lost, my dungeon shook and all my chains fell off."

The only answer to my ineptitude is his attitude. The only answer to my feelings of insufficiency is the certain knowledge of his sufficiency.

The problem of insecurity is widespread. We all suffer from it from time to time. Men would like to say that they don't feel it, but it is not so. There is not a single father who doesn't wonder if he is able to be the provider that his family requires. There is not a man who hasn't, at one time or another, doubted his ability to feed and care for his family. He has wondered, almost daily, what if . . . *What if I lose my job? What if I can't provide for my family? What happens if my children get sick and I can't afford to hire the right set of doctors?*

Men are reluctant sometimes to confess their feelings of inadequacy, but they feel inadequate nonetheless. In the heart of every good Christian father there is a need for Christ, and only that need keeps him living in the arena of trust. Women too feel insecure. What would I do if my husband died or—God forbid—if he left me?

What if I were to lose a child or become incapacitated in some way or could not serve my family?

All of us must ultimately come to God with this question: How do I live out this truth of "Jesus loves me" in the face of all my inadequacies? The answer is simple: I must agree that I am weak and he is strong. I must lift my empty bowl and beg Him to fill it.

EXALTING THE WEAKNESS BY WHICH WE WIN

For me, the most winning passage in the New Testament is Paul's confession of his weakness. Let us consider his words:

> To keep me from being conceited because of these surpassingly great revelations, there was given me a thorn in the flesh, a messenger of Satan, to torment me. Three times I pleaded with the Lord to take it away from me. But he said to me, "My grace is sufficient for you, for my power is made perfect in weakness." Therefore I will boast all the more gladly about my weaknesses, so that Christ's power may rest on me. That is why, for Christ's sake, I delight in weaknesses, in insults, in hardships, in persecutions, in difficul-

ties. For when I am weak, then I am strong. (2
Cor. 12:7–10)

Why would Paul be so utterly thrilled about being so
absolutely helpless? He had learned that swaggering
self-confidence was the fastest route to utter failure. He
had learned that all his bragging ended up in those
condemning feelings of helplessness that tend to
follow failure. On the other hand, when we acknowl-
edge up front that we are weak, we begin to feel we
need such unconquerable certainty with which God
infuses us to keep us from being debilitated by fear and
failure.

One of the best examples of this kind of overcoming
I learned from a friend named Alice who was dying of
cancer. Her disease left her ever weaker as she tra-
versed the last few weeks of her life. She confessed to
me, her pastor, "Every night as I go to sleep, I pray to
the Lord to let me wake up a little stronger than I was
the day before. Alas," she said, "each day I am dis-
turbingly weaker. Yet this I know: carcinoma and God
may be in conflict in my body, but God will win. Cancer
will ultimately lose. You know, Pastor, I am headed to a
land where pain is prohibited, and human weakness
will be forever swallowed up in God's strength."

How right she was. Even as I preached her funeral, I
reminded her friends who gathered there, "Today
cancer lost forever in Alice's life. Today, God won!" Did
I thank God for her cancer? Of course not. Nor was
God happy about the pain she had to live through. But
Alice was determined not to let the momentary pain
steal her ultimate victory.

Paul had a thorn. Did it hurt? Yes. Would he rather
not have had it? Of course. He begged God to take it

from him. But like Alice he woke every morning to find it still in place. But the thorn gave him a sharp sense of focus about the fragile nature of life. He gloried in the empty bowl!

De profundis clamo, the psalmist agonized. "Out of the depths I cry to you" (Ps. 130:1). When there is no other hope, God looms large. Then I can honestly sing, "I am weak, but He is strong" and mean it. The basis of all things good begins in the acknowledgment of our weaknesses.

Alcoholics Anonymous may well be the most healing organization in the world and what is it if not an unhealable gathering of the honest sick. Leper colonies must be filled with closest of friends, for the utter hopelessness of the damned ever welds them into oneness. Father Joseph Damien of Molokai is one of my favorite "holy men." Knowing the eventual cost of his compassion, he went to serve the lepers on the island of Molokai. Loving these pitiable exiles eventually exacted its price. One morning when he was in his kitchen, Damien spilled some scalding water on his foot. When he felt no pain at all, he knew he had become one with those to whom he ministered. The next time Damien stood and addressed his church, he cried out, "My fellow lepers." Their common condition had made them one.

That great missionary statesman D. T. Niles once pictured the whole Christian church as one beggar telling another where he could find bread. We who are Christians are not welded together like a group of entrepreneurs at a *Forbes* magazine awards dinner. No, we are those who found friendship because of our common neediness and our singular confidence in our Supplier.

OUR EXTREMITY IS GOD'S OPPORTUNITY

I have a friend with whom in days past I often prayed. Our place of prayer was his automobile, and we referred to our little tête-à-têtes with God as the "dashboard prayer meetings"! Years ago he confessed to me that he often lamented that he was so busy he felt he just didn't take time to pray and get to know God the way he should.

Not long after this confession, in a late-night accident, he was struck by an oncoming car. His body was catapulted a great distance and slammed into the rock-hard earth. His back was broken in several places and he was told that he might never walk again. In the process of his convalescence he was "pinned and bolted" back together. To facilitate his therapy his young body was suspended in cables and he was left largely naked. He was strapped to a turntable-style bed so he could be clamped and rotated during the long months that his body required to knit back together.

I will never forget visiting him while he was in this lamentable condition. It broke my heart to see his suffering. But he cheered me up with a warm smile, confessing, "You know how I thought I didn't have time to pray? Well, now I do. I'm not going anywhere for the next few months, I think I will use this time to really get to know Jesus."

And so he did.

There are really no substitutes for the confession of sin and the fellowship of need. If I feel sorry for anyone, it must merely be those who swelter under great need and never learn the joy of turning to Christ to find his filling strength. These people never understand that God's greatest gift to us is the empty bowl.

Author Robert Jungk wrote of the unending ordeal of

Claude Eatherly, the American pilot who took part in the bombing of Nagasaki and Hiroshima. His story was first published in the Brussels newspaper *Le Soir* in 1961. After the nuclear weapons fell his story became even more famous because psychiatrist and author Karl Menninger picked it up. I am indebted to him for this account.

Claude Eatherly came back to America a changed man. His friends could hardly recognize him. He had become taciturn and reserved, shunned the company of his fellows. He began to suffer periods of dark depression. In 1947 he received his discharge and returned to his home in Van Alstyne, Texas, refusing the pension he was entitled to. He even wanted to send his medals back to the Pentagon but his friends prevailed upon him to refrain. They could not, however, keep him from expressing his shame and fear at the least mention of Hiroshima. To be called a "war hero" caused him to blush, turn sharply on his heels and walk away. When he was asked about Hiroshima and Nagasaki, his face worked with painful emotion . . .

Eatherly began sending money to the mayor of Hiroshima . . . to be used for the children who had lost their parents in the explosion. He wrote a letter to the municipal council of Hiroshima recounting his part in the bombardment and explaining that it was he who had given the "go ahead" signal and therefore considered himself guilty of the destruction of Hiroshima . . .

He wandered about the country from job to job, started to study but gave it up and took to drink and cards. Nothing could drive out his memories. The "voices" of the Hiroshima victims pursued him incessantly. He would wake up at night crying out for the burning children to be saved. Early in 1950 he tried to commit suicide. Then he decided that he must get himself punished in order to ease his conscience. If society refused to recognize him as a criminal for his part in the bombing of Hiroshima, he reasoned, he must commit some crime recognized as such in the United States. By suffering punishment for that he would expiate his real crime.[4]

Perhaps more than anyone I have ever heard of, Claude Eatherly exhibited what Paul called a "thorn in the flesh." But Paul handled his thorn differently. He used his thorn to help him remember that Christ was his source of healing. Out of Paul's pain came surprising new confidence. His inner struggle ever reminded him that he was weak but Jesus was strong.

I am glad to report that Eatherly at last began to mend. In the years since, he has remembered the critical ratio of life—the comparison of his neediness and smallness to the size of God's all-sufficient largeness.

I am the lord of nothing but my own empty bowl. But this I know: my extremities become God's opportunities.

Many are the lives who were blessed by weaknesses they turned into strength. Solzhenitsyn would cry of his Gulag experience, "Prison, I bless you!" Charles Colson indicates that his national humiliation was but a little price to pay for the Christ he found. Helen Keller felt that her challenges were the very things that created her and she could scarcely do without them. I had a friend who lost his eyesight. He at first despised the darkness but later confessed he had to bless it, for it brought him to a greater dependence on Christ.

Peter affirmed Paul's truth when he said, "To this you were called, because Christ suffered for you, leaving you an example, that you should follow in his steps" (1 Peter 2:21). Of course, Peter went on to say all suffering has a purpose in the life of the Christian. "If you suffer as a Christian, do not be ashamed, but praise God that you bear that name" (1 Peter 4:16). However I feel about my present sufferings, the apostle Paul agreed with Peter when he wrote, "I consider that our present sufferings are not worth comparing to the glory that will be revealed in us" (Rom. 8:18). So I am to let my sufferings become the occasion that God reminds me, and all who watch me suffer, that God has an overcoming agenda with the world and I am indeed "more than [a] conqueror through him who loved [me]" (Rom. 8:37). It all adds up to the glory of the empty bowl in the life of the Christian wise enough to beg God to fill it.

We must celebrate our need—glory in the empty bowl. The bleak winter of our suffering often lies just before the warm spring of splendor.

EGO AND GOD ARE BOTH THREE-LETTER WORDS

I often come to Christ only after I have experienced massive disappointment with myself. I usually try everything I can to save myself. When it's clear I cannot, I cry like Peter, walking the stormy surface of Galilee, "Lord, save me or I perish."

Why? Why do I try everything to save myself before I finally try God? I do so like feeling I did it with no help from anyone anywhere. But most of my self-made drive only forces me into failure and a total loss of self-confidence. I am rather like the run-down soul who went to a psychiatrist confessing that he suffered from low self-esteem. "I wouldn't worry about low self-esteem," said the psychiatrist. "It's common to all losers." I need to remember that the single virtue of low self-esteem is that it readies us to trust the greatness of God.

Confess to God, "Lord, I suffer from an inferiority complex," and you will hear God reply, "Well, of course you do. That's because you are inferior. If you want to be all you can be, trust me and let me fill you with my power. Once I fill your life, you will not be able to feel inferior; all your insufficiency will have been filled with my sufficiency."

Author and evangelist Ian Thomas used to speak of our sufficiency as that of a glove, unfilled by a hand. We can command the glove all day long. But as long as it has no hand inside it, it can perform no service. But fill that glove with a hand and then command it. Then it can grasp, steer a car, lift a weight, comb a child's hair, and hold a Bible.

My life is precisely like this: unfilled by Christ I am at best only a swaggering, pompous ego. At worst I am debilitated by low self-esteem. But filled with Christ then I can serve and stir the very angels to serve my need.

Author Donna Swanson reminds us that Jesus, in becoming a person, understood the difficulties of being human in a world where too often all our difficulties are hard to handle. She asks:

Did you ever cry, Jesus?
Did the world ever pile up on you
   till you wanted to quit?
Did you ever cry, Jesus?
Did you ever get so tired, Jesus,
   you wish you'd never come? . . .
Were you ever lonely, Jesus?

When your friends misunderstood and
  walked out on you, did you ever cry, Jesus?
I think you must have,
  for I know you so well. So well!
I think you must have cried a little.[5]

Indeed we know that Jesus wept at times. He wept when his friends thought he couldn't raise Lazarus (John 11:35). He wept when he saw the citizens of Jerusalem living pointlessly for themselves (Luke 19:41). He seems to weep in Gethsemane when his entire body was sweating great drops of blood (Luke 22:44).

Yet what was the difference between the way he wept and the way I do it? I usually cry when I find I have failed. I cry as evidence that I could not live up to my own expectations. But Jesus cried because those who were his friends preferred to serve their own egos and live powerless, empty lives. He wept because those who claimed to love him refused to be filled with his strength. It is a crying matter for God when I choose to be a weak display of all that he wants to achieve through my life.

CONCLUSION

So then, how am I to view my circumstances? Thomas à Kempis said that I should never pray to have more friends and softer circumstances. He said I am to pray that I have trials and antagonists, for when I have only enemies will I retreat of necessity to the bosom of Christ.

Charles Spurgeon said, "Look to the living One for life. Look to Jesus for all you need between the gate of

Hell and the gate of Heaven."[6] How true his advice; by looking in such a way I can remember his strength and my weakness.

When missionary Hudson Taylor's wife lay dying, their blessed romance was coming to a close in terms of their earthly existence. Yet they endured the passing with great affection:

> "My darling, are you conscious that you are dying?"
>
> "Dying? Do you think so? What makes you think so?"
>
> "I can see it, Darling."
>
> "What is making me die?"
>
> "Your strength is giving way."
>
> "Can it be so? I feel no pain, only weakness."
>
> "Yes, you are going home. You will soon be with Jesus."
>
> "I am sorry . . ."
>
> "You are not sorry to go to be with Jesus?"
>
> "I cannot be sorry to go to Him . . . But it does grieve me to leave you alone at such a time. Yet . . . He will be with you and meet all your needs."[7]

Shortly after this she sank ever lower physically and died. But Hudson Taylor recommitted his life to Christ, to serve him faithfully and alone. Her passing was the edge of extremity that brought the empowering Christ back into Taylor's life for the saving of China.

Theologian Dietrich Bonhoeffer spoke a lot about the necessity of differentiating between cheap and costly grace. Costly grace was grace that was appropriated at the cost of our own debilitation. God's opportunity almost always begins in our extremities.

The weakness with which I must face my world need

never force me to live a limited life of dissipation. He longs to fill me with his strength. How is this to be done? I arm myself in his strength when I dissolve my frailty in his power. It is—as almost all of the great contemplatives wrote—a matter of my union with Christ.

Who knows how many have been encouraged in this way by the simple yet deep life of Brother Lawrence? He was not a complex man with a complex plan. His simple neediness he learned in a monastery kitchen. There, and not in the prayer cell, he made friends with God. He wrote his words for the completion of our needy glory: "The time of business does not with me differ from the time of prayer; and in the noise and clatter of my kitchen, while several persons are at the same time calling for different things, I possess God in as great tranquility as if I were upon my knees at the blessed sacrament."[8]

How I learn such dependency has nothing to do with my environment or my capacity for spiritual depth. It has only to do with my hunger.

My strength has nothing to do with my capabilities, only with my Christ-reliance.

It is hunger that teaches me to eat. To be sure, etiquette may help me choose a fork and hold a teacup. But hunger is the grand instructor. In January 1982 in a time of spiritual barrenness I wrote these words.

Come thou World-lover, Thou Mighty within!
Small whisper resound and be born as a shout!
Deep hunger be thunder . . . and wash me again
Inside me grow strong, then turn inside out.

Teach me my weaknesses until I exalt in your strength. I lift an empty bowl and I wait.

QUESTIONS FOR REFLECTION

1. In what ways is the symbol of the "beggar's bowl" a contrast between our need and God's sufficiency?

2. In what ways have you found the statement "Confession is the basis of all valid relationships" to be true or untrue?

3. Explain why you believe the statement "Coming clean in God's presence is the only hope I have of living clean before him."

4. Ted Bundy described an addiction that he felt was critically responsible for his serial murders. Have you ever known anyone who was a slave to the kind of captivity he describes? Did you try to help that person? If so, how?

5. Have you ever known anyone whom you felt was destroyed by his or her addictions? What steps do you take in your life to be sure that none of your appetites ever become your master?

6. Do you think that men or women are more reluctant to be honest about their spiritual needs? Why is it important to be open about our spiritual neediness?

7. Why does Paul seems so happy about his "thorn in the flesh" in 2 Corinthians 12:7–10?

8. Why did Alexander Solzhenitsyn, in speaking of his Gulag experiences, cry, "Prison I bless, you!"?

9. Why did Jesus weep when those he loved refused to be filled with his strength?

10. What does this statement mean to you: "The weakness with which I must face my world need never force me to live a limited life of dissipation."

CHAPTER 8

He Who Died, Heaven's Gate to Open Wide

If the Father deigns to touch with divine power the cold and pulse-less heart of the buried acorn and to make it burst forth from its prison walls, will He leave neglected in the earth the soul of man, made in the image of the Creator? If He stoops to give to the rose-bush, whose withered blossoms float upon the autumn breeze, the sweet assurance of another springtime, will He refuse the words of hope to the sons of men when the frosts of winter come? If matter, mute and inanimate, though changed by the forces of nature into a multitude of forms, can never die, will the spirit of man suffer anni-hilation when it has paid a brief visit like a royal guest to this tene-ment of clay? No, I am as sure that there is another life as I am that I live today.

In Cairo I secured a few grains of wheat that had slumbered for more than three thousand years in an Egyptian tomb. As I looked at them this thought came into my mind: If one of those grains had been planted on the banks of the Nile the year after it grew, and all its lineal descendents planted and replanted from that time until now, its progeny would today be sufficiently numerous to feed the teeming millions of the world. There is in the grain of wheat an invisible something which has power to discard the body that we see, and from earth and air fashion a new body so much like the old one that we cannot tell the one from the other. If this invisible germ of life in the grain of wheat can thus pass unimpaired through three thousand resurrections, I shall not doubt that my soul has power to clothe itself with a body suited to its new exis-tence when this earthly frame has crumbled into dust.

WILLIAM JENNINGS BRYAN[1]

A CONVERSATION WITH JESUS

Lord, was your cross all that necessary?

Yes—it's why I came. The Son of man did not come to be served; he came to give his life as a ransom for many. You may be sure that if there had been any other way to save you I would not have chosen the cross.

Why? Why die? Wouldn't it be better just to live, own a home, raise a family, and make a good living? Aren't these the things that make for the good life?

The good life is not bought with silver—nor guaranteed by gold. The good life has one definition—knowing we are loved by God. So merely having things is not the good life. A man's life does not consist in the abundance of things he possesses.

But isn't it always better to live and do good than to be dead and do nothing?

Living is not always the way to do good. The human race found heaven brought near in my dying. Commit your life to God's keeping if you would do the best good. For whoever wants to save his life will lose it, but whoever loses his life for my sake will find it.

I know you love your followers but wouldn't you rather hang around and live with them and for them than to suffer and die for them?

No, all that lives must die and it is only in the dying that real life becomes possible. Except a grain of wheat be willing to die, it cannot free the tiny plant within it. So I too must die. I am the Good Shepherd, and the Good Shepherd lays down his life for the sheep.

But how in simply dying can you really prove you love me?

Dying is the last great gift that may be given. Greater love hath no man than this, that he lay down his life for his friends.

Very well, if you are resigned.

I am resigned. It is finished! I am the resurrection and the life. He that believes in me, though he were dead, yet shall he live. There is no other way but the cross. None! For this reason I was born; for this reason I came into the world. I am the way, the truth, and the life. No man comes unto the Father but by me.

Matthew 20:28; Luke 12:15; Matthew 16:25; John 10:11; John 15:13; John 11:25; John 18:37; John 14:6

The number-one fear of aging people is the sheer terror of living a meaningless life.[2] Throughout my years as a pastor I heard this repeated lament from the manic souls who came my way: "What have I ever done? . . . I have done nothing . . . What do I mean to my world? . . . I mean nothing!"

Behind this dismal rhetoric is a common quest. We are all embroiled in a search for our significance. Oddly, we do not gain significance by trying to achieve a set of goals. We achieve significance in accepting the fact we are loved. I came as a child upon the wonder of God's grace. I was astounded by the fact that Jesus loved me. I was loved for no reason except I had a soul and God, for reasons that still baffle me, was crazy about me. "Jesus loves me! He who died Heaven's gate to open wide." God's love swung open heaven's gate, and when the gate swung wide I had significance. Still, I could see that while I meant a great deal to God, I also had to find meaning in myself.

In my childhood an old philosopher told me, "Thrust your hand down into a pail of water. When you see the hole that's left when you draw it out, you will see the impression your life has made on your world." Most of us from time to time know the horrible fear of dying as one ordinary soul—a statistical cipher in the swarm of the human average. I am ever haunted by a cartoon of a look-alike penguin leaping up in joy from a flock of his clones, saying, "I gotta be me."

Frank Sinatra sang the anthem that lies at the center of all ego-driven personhood: "I did it my way." And how was his way different? What made his way so unique that he sang an anthem to it? In reality it looked pretty much like everyone else's way. He got his four-score years, ate a little, drank a little, died a little, and was dead.

There's an inherent nihilism that dogs the best of our dreams. The Book of Ecclesiastes is a heart-cry for human bondage. We are all dying on our way to being dead. Dying is not so much a point as it is a process. We do some of it every day until it is all done.

A part of Jesus' agenda was to strike death from the human agenda. As the child's hymn reminds us, he loved us enough to open the gate of heaven—the gate of eternity, the gate of significance. He is our great raison d'être, our reason to be. None who come into contact with him will ever have to confess that they found no reason for their existence.

When I was a child, James Forrestal leapt from the eighth floor of the Naval Hospital in Bethesda, Maryland, taking his life. His "Good-bye, cruel world" note contained the haunting words of Sophocles:

> *When reason's day sets rayless, joyless*
> *Quenched in cold decay,*
> *'Tis better to die than linger on*
> *And try to live when the soul's life is gone.*

Yes, Jesus loves me, and he who died—heaven's gate to open wide—is my security in the face of death. This is the exalted theme of the Easter Scriptures. Christianity begins to live where its Founder died. Jesus spoke of wildflowers, but wildflowers never rose to become the central symbol of our faith. He spoke of bread, but brazen loaves do not crown our steeple tops. Our symbol is the cross. Even little children can see the death of Christ as the starting place of faith.

Of the 365 days that comprise my year, I am struck silent on Good Friday and set to rejoicing on Easter. And these days preface and conclude a weekend of wonder. I am lovestruck by majesty and I go about singing

> *Alas! and did my Savior bleed?*
> *And did my sovereign die?*
> *Would He devote that sacred head*
> *For such a worm as I?*[3]

I have watched the old hymn surrender up its "wormy" theology. It is now sung, "Would he devote that sacred head for sinners such as I?" But I leave the "worm" in it when I sing it. "Worm" speaks louder of my need for grace and more of my wonder for a God who stoops quite a distance to save.

CRUCIFIXION CONFIDENCE

The cross has become a symbol of the almighty love that created the church and its method of creating the church is human transformation.

But all who realize the purpose of his dying see it as a demonstration of his saving love. The ultimate power of that love—as the children's hymn has it—was to "open wide" heaven's gate.

At the cross comes a great divorce. I cannot accept what happened there in two modes. I must either see a naked evildoer and criminal from whom I turn my eyes in shame, or I must see the sinless sacrifice of God.

When I see him in this latter way I am compelled to fall on my face before his fearless and achieving love. In my penitence, I am changed by his dying.

In churches the cross is often presented one of three ways. First, it is presented as a crucifix, on which an image of the dying Savior hangs suspended. Evangelicals often react negatively to crucifixes, pointing out they are adorned by a dead, metal Jesus. They prefer the empty cross, saying that Jesus is alive; to see the empty cross ought to remind us also that the gate of heaven stands wide open. I never grow weary of a crucifix, though, at least conceptually. Of course I never kiss them nor ask these pewter saviors to deal with my problems. Still, in my heart of hearts, I know that my most serious problems were solved when Jesus died.

Christ gave me two kinds of dignity when he died. First of all, my own death will one day make sense. I've yet to grapple with death but I know it looms out ahead of me. It grows closer with each approaching decade. Yet every time I catch a glimpse of the crucified Christ lifted up above my petty problems, I say to myself, *If Jesus could die naked for humankind, then no kind of dying has to be without nobility.*

His passing from this present world causes us to seek a richer meaning in all finality. We want "to inhale every sunrise and look under every rock for the joy life has to offer."[4] Dying is so much more purposeful for all of us because Jesus died the way he did.

But not only did Jesus give our dying dignity, he also gave purpose to our living. Usually the most discouraging lives are spent giving life 100 percent with no concept of where they are going. Author and humorist Don Herold said, "Unhappiness is in not knowing what we want and killing ourselves to get it."[5] But happiness comes in living "the crucified life." Paul said his own life purpose came from being "crucified with Christ" (Gal. 2:20). I don't know what this means, but I like to think of it this way: when I'm involved in some big-deal project, I stop and ask myself, *If I were dying on a cross beside Jesus, right now, would what I fidget over be really all that important?* Then I appropriate the richest meaning of the cross! Jesus' dying gilds my life with significance in the now. But he also gilds our future with significance; it is he who died, heaven's gate to open wide.

A second way the cross is presented is wearing the letters "I.H.S"—an abbreviation for *In Hoc Signo (Vinces)* or "By this sign (the cross) you will conquer." According to tradition Constantine saw a vision of a burning fiery cross and was given this "I.H.S." message from God. This Latin assurance was given to the Roman general to assure him he would win the Roman civil war by serving the cross of Christ. According to some historians, he then painted crosses on all his shields, won the war, and became the first Christian emperor.

But what does *I.H.S.* mean to me in the day-to-day living of my life? I am guided into the best lifestyle by placing my every moral action under the sign of the cross. One of the worthy books I cherish is Jean Pierre De Cassaude's *Sacrament of the Present Moment.* This scholar has taught me I can sanctify—make holy—my every moment by lifting the cross above every difficulty I face. *In Hoc Signo* then becomes my way of saying to every choice I make, "I now sanctify my ordinary clock and give this hour of the day unto God for whatever purpose he will make of it." So what makes me feel every moment is worth the sanctifying? Just as Christ owns me, he also owns the present moment. Therefore I may cry *"In Hoc Signo"* and go after life with perfect confidence that God is taking care of me. His death makes the future as certain as the present. Earth's gate is open to my opportunity, heaven's gate is open to my eternity.

Mother Teresa of Calcutta almost suggests that I may sanctify my present moment only by interacting with that moment. In such a way, then, the clock no longer bores me but entices me to action. It calls me to become authentic by electing to choose how I shall spend each moment of my life. How I choose to spend life tells me what I mean to God.

> What we are doing is but a drop in the ocean. This may be only a drop, but the ocean would be less if it weren't there. What we do is something small, but we do it with big hearts. At death, we will not be judged by the amount of work we did, but by the amount of love we put into it. We do not strive for spectacular actions. What counts is the gift of yourself, the degree of love you put into each of your deeds . . . Do you want to be great? Pick up a broom and sweep the floor.[6]

The point is that whatever I do, I must act in the moment and in the name of Christ to give the moment meaning. The *I.H.S.* sanctifies the entire calendar of all who serve the cross. Under this sign I will pick up a broom and become real in a world where arrogance despises to serve.

The third way the cross of Christ is presented is with another set of Latin letters, "I.N.R.I." These letters are an abbreviation of the *titulus*—the sign that hung over Jesus' cross listing the reason he was crucified. I.N.R.I. stands for *Iesus Nazarenus Rex Iudaeorum* or "Jesus of Nazareth, King of the Jews." At his trial, Jesus' enemies asked the Roman governor, Pilate, not to put a sign over his cross saying "King of the Jews." Instead, they counseled Pilate to write, "He *said* he was King of the Jews" (see John 19:21). If his accusers had achieved their goal they would have diminished Jesus' claims. But Pilate refused their counsel and these simple four letters stood over the cross, insisting that Jesus was who he said he was.

King Jesus! When I say these words I confess I am a servant. Greatness, perhaps even fame, rarely originates in either heredity or environment. It is born when I catch a view of what I can do or am willing to become often by serving Christ in the most mundane of circumstances.

But I must not see myself as special. To do so is to deny Christ's total control of my life. The most extraordinary people never saw themselves as great. In fact many of them struggle against a negative group opinion. Albert Einstein for instance, didn't talk till he was four years old and he didn't start to read till he was seven. One of his teachers labeled him as "mentally slow, unsociable and adrift in his foolish dreams." Thomas Edison was considered "too stupid to learn anything," said some of his teachers. The rookie coach Vince Lombardi was said to possess minimal football knowledge and to lack motivation. Walt Disney was fired by a local newspaper because he had a "lack of fresh ideas."[7]

What is it that changed these ordinary souls into icons of heroism? Their inner view was strong enough to stand against their belittling critics.

I found that Christ performs just such a service in my life.

REWRITING MY AUTOBIOGRAPHY

As a Christian I am not asked merely to believe there was a Jesus, but that he acted to save me by dying in my stead. I dare not present him as some kind of Santa Claus sent out to give me the gift of life at no real cost to himself. I need not become gruesome in describing the cross, but I must never be dishonest in cherishing the most beautiful truth of my faith.

Author Joseph Wittig once said all biographies in a sense should begin by examining the person's death, because only from the standpoint of the end of our lives can all of our lives be seen in perspective.

Robert Frost made the same statement in his poem "Two Tramps in Mud Time":

My object in living is to write
my avocation and my vocation
as my two eyes make one in sight.
Only where love and need are one . . .
and the work is play for mortal stakes
is the deed ever really done for heaven
and the future's sakes.[8]

Jesus' death reminds me that I too will die and I ought never live too far from this remembrance. Why? Because my contemplation of the time when I will be no more makes me the best possible steward of the present moment.

For years one of my favorite verses of Scripture has been "Teach us to number our days, that we may apply our hearts unto wisdom" (Ps. 90:12 KJV). The clock of my life is ticking. Time hurries and will eventually outrun me. What will I look like when time goes on without me? Robert Frost reminds me I matter only where the work and play are "for mortal stakes." Only then are my deeds really done for heaven.

I have an aging friend who is a hardware salesman. All of his adult life he has represented various hardware wholesalers in marketing their wares to retail stores. "When you die," I asked, "why will you say you have lived?"

He pointed to the three portraits of his three sons proudly displayed on his office wall. "I was born for three reasons. I have given my life to offer the world these three best proofs of why I was ever born. Look at them, are they not worthy?" I looked at them—they were bright, handsome, and achievers as this world can know achievement.

I believe my own mother felt that same way about me. Sometimes when I feel my work has no great import and that my service has been all overlooked, I try to remember I was her reason to reckon with Psalm 90:12 and to say, "I have numbered my days—I have a son—I have not lived in vain."

In a way, I am her *tetelestai.* This Greek verb was one of Jesus' seven final words. It means, "It is finished!" Jesus died winning! He died with every aspect of why he was born completely satisfied.

So it is with the cross. Only by watching Jesus die can I tell how well he lived out all the things he said in life. For instance, when he said he was "the truth" (John 14:6), he really meant it. In a way Christ died for refusing to lie his way out of all he was accused of being at his trial. It would have been a simple matter to avoid his execution. When Pilate said, "Are you God?" he could have laughed and said, "Get real! Do I look like God?" He might have backed down from the truth and avoided execution. But he was the sinless Son of God, so he clung to truth and died.

THE DRAMA OF SELF-DENIAL

Jesus spoke often of self-denial. He was thirty-three years old and the picture of health. He had achieved a brisk level of warm popularity. Of course he wanted to avoid dying. He asked God in Gethsemane not to let him die, if there was any other way to serve him. God told him there was no other way.

Jesus reminded the disciples that he did not want to die. He was dying to honor his Father, who was so in love with the human race he volunteered his Son for this bold plan of redemption, "Heaven's gate to open wide."

Jesus died serving truth and the truth bears heavy requirements. Ernest Becker, in his Pulitzer Prize–winning *The Denial of Death*, says our age is one in which people "deny their deaths" by either worshiping a hero or trying to become one. Whichever is the issue, heroes and their stories have also become a vehicle for theology. In our time, or within easy reach of it, have lived such noble souls as Mohandas Gandhi, Martin Luther King Jr., and other sociological heroes. Author James W. McClendon suggests that within these oft-Christlike figures emerge visible virtues of self-sacrifice. In other words, they are like Jesus, living and dying for reasons beyond themselves.

Dag Hammarskjöld was one of these. His life bore an elegant, Christlike witness. Hammarskjöld, secretary general of the United Nations, was killed in a plane crash in Katanga while on a U.N. peace-keeping mission in 1961. After his death, his now famous journals were discovered and published under the title of *Markings*. He wrote his own definition of what it means to die so others might live: "A jealous dream which refuses to share you with anybody or anything else: the greatest creation of mankind—the dream of mankind. The greatest creation of mankind, in which it is the noblest dream of the individual—to lose himself. Therefore: gladly death or humiliation if that is what the dream demands."[9]

The crucifixion was heaven's great dream for the future of the human race. How does this dream speak to Jesus' death? Somewhat adequately, for Hammarskjöld said that this one dream unites such Christian tenets as "death, destiny, sacrifice and forgiveness."[10]

Jesus died to release within me the power of the finest life I might hope for. Jesus as an inner force reminds me that I belong to God for God's purposes. The death of Christ constantly reminds me that Jesus had no selfish moments in which he lounged about in his own hedonistic dreams of how he could best get on in this world.

An old Russian fable lends insight to the cross. Once upon a time—near the era when 1899 was stumbling into 1900—a rabbi wandered about the city debating the wisdom of trusting in God. He wrangled over his call to the ministry and doubted for a moment some of the great truths of Scripture. Distracted by the freezing air that seeped into his frigid doubt, he wandered— quite by accident—into a czarist military compound. It was at this point that his despairing reverie was interrupted by the blatant call of a black-booted sentry: "Who are you? What are you doing here?"

"Excuse me," begged the stunned rabbi.

"Who are you? What are you doing here?" repeated the sentry.

The rabbi shook himself to clear the cobwebs from his mind. Then he stared at the soldier and asked, "My good sentry, how much do you get paid every day?"

"What does that have to do with your illegal entry to this post?"

"Sir, you have awakened me from a doubtful heart with life's two most important questions. I promise to pay you a sum equal to your military salary if you will ask me those same two questions every day."

"What two questions?" asked the dumbfounded sentry.

"Who are you and what are you doing here?"

These are indeed the two most important questions. I cannot think of Jesus' dying without asking myself who I am and what I am doing on the planet. All that we ought to be and all we are called to do becomes clear when we consider the price he paid.

THE GRAND GATE

The second phrase of this line from "Jesus Loves Me" reminds me that in dying, he opened heaven's gate. How so? In his dying, Jesus exposed the once-hidden aspects of God's redemption, making them visible to all ages. The cross became the draw-cord of those drapes that hid the deep things of God. The word *apocalypse* is our English transliteration of the Greek word that means "revelation." The word means literally to "bring out of hiding" or "a drawing of the drapes." It's what happens when the orchestra finishes the overture, the tympani rolls, and the cymbals clash. Then the drapes part and the audience sees for the first time the glorious stage setting of Act One.

Jesus died, the thunder rolled, and the drapes were opened. There stood open to all the best of the long-hidden attributes of God. The gospel writer Luke says that when Jesus died the literal curtain in the temple (see Luke 23:45) was torn in two (and perhaps thrown back) to reveal the once-hidden Holy of Holies. In that holy but sunless room, where only the high priest went once a year, sat the ark of the covenant. There the faithful worshipers believed that God dwelt specially in all his fullness.

But God came out of hiding in Jesus. The privacy was gone. Jesus in dying revealed the innermost heart of God. And the child's hymn says that beyond the tearing of the temple curtain, heaven's gate was opened wide. How wide? The entire Book of Revelation is a glistening description of all that's been happening in heaven since the Son of God reentered it. Now his hiddenness is our common joy: we know Jesus is there. He has died. Heaven's gate is wide open. We have access to his presence forever.

I had a dear friend who strangled in the unrelenting pain of cancer. Day by day her disease wrapped its ever-extending tentacles of death around her life. She fought the beast with chemicals and radium until the dragon won and her endless shots of morphine faded into streets of gold. I must confess that at her funeral all I could say was, "Free, free, free at last."

Heaven is the grand liberation.

Freedom is the final count. He had suffered much for the sake of the gospel. He desired nothing more than to be free. He desired, as the child's hymn says, for heaven's gate to be opened wide.

GOD'S VALENTINE TO THE WORLD

Jesus died and his cross is both a welcome-home invitation and a divine valentine. He really did die, "Heaven's gate to open wide." Edmond John Carnell testified to this reality when he wrote: "As death draws near and we dread the dark journey ahead, the Lord will assure us that our lives are precious in the sight of God. He will gently say, 'Child, come home.' Jesus has given his word that he will never leave us or forsake us, and his word is as firm as his character."[11]

The homecoming, however, is by invitation only. The key to God's holy invitation is our faith in Christ. But the invitation is shrouded in the mystery of God's grace.

Still, the fact that his love is shrouded in mystery should never lead us to conclude that his promises are uncertain. It is not so. His grace is a mystery because it is past all understanding. But it is as real as the universe itself. It is a mystery that gives us a planet to live on and never feels compelled to explain itself.

It is clear we will present this invitation to God upon our final breath as we join the grand reunion of all saints. But we dare not miss the simpler glory of the here and now that precedes the grander final glory. He issued the invitation and opened heaven's gate because he loved us. He died for us because he loved us. The cross is a kind of divine valentine given to all to remind us we are loved.

Charles Swindoll, president of Dallas Theological Seminary, tells a poignant story about a physically challenged child who was often abused and always ignored by his classmates. The little boy wanted to be sure that he participated fully in the giving and receiving of valentines. On the day of the valentine exchange he took his bag of cards to school. He was excited that he had made out a card for everyone in the class.

That day, although the kids each received a valentine from him, he received none. The children had conspired in a terrible cruelty and agreed not to give him any cards.

On the way home that night the boy walked along, muttering "Not one, not one, not a single one." He continued this recitation till he was home. When his mother asked him what he was saying he spoke up, "Not one, Mama! Not one! I didn't forget a single one. I gave everybody a valentine."

This is the all-inclusive lesson of the cross. No one is forgotten in the cross. Jesus loves us so much, he must surely have entered heaven saying, "Not one, not a single one. My blood has covered all. No one has been left out."

Recently I began meditating on the inequalities of life. Sometimes it seems to me that some of the world's secret heroes have died and been buried with very little acknowledgment. An English princess and a young, handsome magazine editor are buried with great pomp while some of God's greatest saints, having given God all, die unacknowledged. But Jesus has died and has invited us to consider a world where the ultimate saints are those who die in self-denial, not in self-indulgence. For all who die in Christ, heaven's gate is open wide. Love has faced death and destroyed it.

CONCLUSION

Someday I will stand at the grand opening of heaven's gate and remember the wonderful story of the angels. It is said that when Jesus left heaven to come to earth, the gates swung open to let him pass in order that he might be born in Bethlehem. As he left, the angels were bright with joy. Gabriel asked, "Where are you going, Lord?"

"To earth to save human beings," answered Jesus.

The angels broke into applause at the triumph of such a wonderful quest.

But they were all still standing there thirty-three years later as Jesus returned through the gates. His face was scarred and torn, his back lacerated by the whip, his hands torn by the steel.

"Lord," cried the angels, "what happened? Did you save humankind?"

"Not all of them," said Jesus. "Only 120 or so. They are all gathered now, praying for the coming of the Spirit."

"Only 120? What about all the rest of humankind?" cried the angels.

"This 120 must tell the others or the rest of the world will never be saved."

"But, Lord," the angels insisted, "what if they don't tell the others?"

"Then I have no other plans."

That is where the fable ends, but I like thinking that as Jesus passed on through the open gate, the angels began to pull them shut to lock them up behind him and prevent anyone from the cruel planet that had killed Jesus ever to enter the realm of light.

But Jesus, on seeing them drawing the gate, stopped and turned and cried,

> *Let the gates stand open wide*
> *For I the planet's crucified*
> *Have loved the needy world and died.*

QUESTIONS FOR REFLECTION

1. How do you relate to the chapter's opening statement that the number-one fear people have is the "sheer terror of having lived a meaningless life"? What do you consider your best offering to the world? What gives you the feeling that you are contributing to God's world in a significant way?

2. In what way does Christ's dying give hope and meaning to our own? What is it that you most admire in the way Jesus handled the ordeal of dying?

3. Do you agree that you can never really tell how well people have lived until you've had the opportunity to see how they faced their own deaths? If you do agree, can you think of a friend or relative who died victoriously even under difficult circumstances? What did you most admire about how he or she handled the circumstances?

4. How would you apply Psalm 90:12 to your own life?

5. What does it mean to say that in Christ, love faced death and destroyed it?

6. The cross is the drapery cord that drew the curtains back to expose the world's greatest truth: that the tragedy of dying is not as significant as the life Christ won in the process. Put this in your own words.

7. What does the following statement mean to you: "The cross is a kind of divine valentine given to all of us to remind us we are loved."

CHAPTER 9

He Will Wash Away My Sin, Let His Little Child Come In

For my own part, I have never ceased to rejoice that God has appointed me to such an office. People talk of the sacrifice I have made in spending so much of my life in Africa. Can that be called a sacrifice which is simple interest paid back as a small part of a great debt owing to our God, which we can never repay? Is that a sacrifice which brings its own blest reward in healthful activity, the consciousness of doing good, peace of mind, and a bright hope of a glorious destiny hereafter? Away with the word in such a view, and with such a thought! It is emphatically no sacrifice. Say rather it is a privilege. Anxiety, sickness, suffering, or danger, now and then, with a foregoing of the common conveniences and charities of this life, may make us pause, and cause the spirit to waver, and the soul to sink; but let this be only for a moment. All these are nothing when compared with the glory which shall hereafter be revealed in, and for, us. I never made a sacrifice. Of this we ought not to talk, when we remember the great sacrifice which He made who left His Father's throne on high to give Himself for us; "who being the brightness of that Father's glory, and the express image of his person, and upholding all things by the word of his power, when he had by himself purged our sins, sat down on the right hand of the Majesty on high."

DAVID LIVINGSTON[1]

A CONVERSATION WITH JESUS

Jesus, sin is a term our culture seems to have out-grown. No one would call anyone else a "sinner." Isn't it true that we live in an enlightened culture that's outgrown sin? Hasn't the world vetoed the very notion?

There is none good, only God. If the world should state that the oceans do not exist, would this change the world? To rule that sin does not exist changes nothing. All have sinned and come short of the glory of God.

Then if this is so why isn't God more tolerant of sin? Why should God be so against such a universal affliction?

Can we be tolerant of the plague merely because it's epidemic? Can we forgive a massacre because so many die? Sin is a universal killer, and it requires an all-powerful God to deal with such a widespread horror. Therefore, the soul that sins must die, and I have paid the sacrifice for sin once and for all.

But how can we be sure that if we confess our sin God will forgive us?

Understand this: The angels wait at rapt attention to hear any needy soul beg for my redemption. When anyone cries "Forgive!" angelic anthems roar throughout the cosmos. It is heaven's glory! So, if

anyone confesses sins I am faithful and just to forgive
those sins and to cleanse from all unrighteousness.

*How was it you were given such power—the power to
forgive all who ask for it?*

This is why I came, to deal with sin—to save sinners, not the righteous. Tell everyone the Good News
that they have been forgiven. For I myself have borne
everyone's sins in my body on the tree so that all sinners might die to their waywardness. Thus I wait for
all to cry and then my dying will have meaning.
Then the cross is the seal of our love. Blessed are all
who understand their sin is real. When they turn to
me in repentance I will send the warm love of heaven
to embrace their honesty and teach them to enjoy
the clean, brisk air of holiness.

ROMANS 3:23; MATTHEW 9:13

Joan of Arc's "voices" first came to her with a very simple charge: "Be a good girl and go to church." I have found that God rarely trusts me with big assignments until I have learned the simple art of obedience in smaller matters. I must see my sin as serious. Yet Jesus washes away our sin and until we take it seriously we shall likely not get to any advanced relationship with God.

The things I do wrong hurt God. In some mystical way I understand that my sins are responsible for all that Jesus endured on the cross. Hence all my life I have been trapped between my inability to stop sinning and my constant need to be forgiven. Thus I remain a lifelong debtor to grace.

In our time, *sin* seems a short, funny word. It smacks of frontier revivalism and high-button shoes. While it is a frequent word in Scripture, it is no longer heard much in churches. So what can it mean to say "He will wash away my sin"? Just this: sin is what Jesus used to save us from, back before he began to save us from low self-esteem and poor stock investments. Sin for swanky postmoderns seems only an old Salvation Army doctrine preached to bleary-eyed people who just stopped by to hear the street brass. Nobody in recent years even admits to it. The word *sinful* was once considered to be an important part of theology but of late is only an adjective we apply to gooey desserts and rooftop restaurants.

The last serious psychologist to bring the word up was Karl Menninger, who wrote *Whatever Happened to Sin?* Nobody much responded to his question and it died for lack of an answer. But it must be remembered that Menninger wrote his book on a wave of happy-go-lucky, self-improvement, psychological thrillers such as *I'm OK, You're OK* and *Games People Play.* At that time the school of Transactional Analysis was teaching that all bad behavior (much of which was previously called *sin)* could be explained by examining our social transactions and hearing those three inner voices (parent, adult, child) that could be broken down to explain all errant behavior. Sin was not something we did to offend God. It was merely a glitch in relationships—a breakdown in the way people got along. In time this popular view of wrong became so firmly established that *sin* dropped completely out of our vocabulary. Finally, in our own time, has arisen the bumper-sticker ethics of our new morality: "Hurt no one, and do what you please."

Augustine said, "Love God, and do what you please." Both Augustine and current bumper stickers are expressing ways to be free, but Augustine's way offers freedom in finding a focus on loving God, while the bumper sticker offers freedom by encouraging folks to forget about God.

I often meet people who, having bypassed God, are in a dreadful sweat to forgive their own sins. Most of the time they manage this by comparing themselves with people even worse than they are. Early on I formed the habit of comparing myself with Jesus—the sinless Son of God. Alas, I could never arrive at any form of self-congratulation by doing this.

I'm a fan of the comic strip *B.C.* precisely because the artist, Johnny Hart, is forever asking theological questions for which few, if any, of us have a very satis-factory answer. In one of his cartoons Wiley is under a primeval tree with his stone wax tablet writing his puz-zlement over our natural propensity to sin:

Why do people go to the trouble
Why do they bust someone's bubble
When they know it comes back to them double
Why do we go to the trouble to hurt
Someone we actually love . . .
Why can't we overlook others' mistakes
We've all surely been there before
Love and forgiveness is all that it takes
To boot Satan's rear out the door.[2]

Johnny Hart seems to imply that Augustine's view is better than that of the bumper sticker. Why? Because loving God carries with it the powerful implication that God loves everyone and desires the best possible life for all. God demonstrates no human preferences of making some people his special friends while pushing others to the side. God can't be bought off with special interest, partisanship, or political arrangements. Loving God mandates that we love everyone whom God loves. We cannot claim to love God while we keep our petulant, specialized grudges toward others. The apostle John said, "If anyone says 'I love God,' yet hates his brother, he is a liar. For anyone who does not love his brother, whom he has seen, cannot love God, whom he has not seen" (1 John 4:20–21). John seems to agree with Augustine when he says, "Whoever loves God must also love his brother" (1 John 4:21). And if this be true, the issue of the bumper sticker is resolved. I cannot hurt anyone if I love God, for to really love God is to surrender all vicious self-interest.

So it is true that he who loves does indeed wash away our sin. More than that, in Christ our circle of loving is complete, helping us ever to end where we started. Loving God is the single passion that keeps me from sinning and as I avoid sinning I find myself even more rapt in loving God. My focus on love can then sanctify my world by doing one thing at a time and doing all for the Glory of God. Jean Pierre De Caussade wrote of it this way:

Is not a picture painted on a canvas by the application of one stroke of the brush at a time? Similarly the cruel chisel destroys a stone with each cut. But what the stone suffers by repeated blows is no less than the shape the mason is making of it. And should a poor stone be asked, "What is happening to you?" it might reply "Don't ask me. All I know is that for my part there is nothing for me to know or do, only to remain steady under the hand of my master and to love him and suffer him to work out my destiny. It is for him to know and to achieve this. I know neither what he is doing nor why. I only know that he is doing what is best and most perfect, and I suffer each cut of the chisel as though it were the best thing for me, even though, to tell the truth, each one is my idea of ruin, destruction and defacement. But ignoring all this, I rest contented with the present moment. Thinking only of my duty to it, I submit to the work of this skillful master without caring to know what it is."[3]

TO WILL ONE THING

Indeed there may be only one sin for those who believe in Christ. It is the sin of knowing Christ but not holding his acquaintance special. It is the sin of trying to love both Christ and something else. This sin splits the human soul in two by dividing the love we ought to give only to God so that we spend part of our affection somewhere else. In Deuteronomy 5:8–9 the Lord reminded all of Israel: "You shall not make for yourself an idol of anything in heaven above or on the earth beneath or in the waters below. You shall not bow down to them or worship them; for I, the LORD your God, am a jealous God, punishing the children for the sin of the fathers to the third and fourth generation of those who hate me."

God will not tolerate my serving two gods at once. Every polygamy of the heart is regarded as idolatry in heaven. For me, sin begins in setting God alongside any other object of my adoration and trying to love them both equally.

Gleb Nerzhin is the protagonist of Solzhenitsyn's novel *The First Circle*. Solzhenitsyn states the struggle in his hero's life in this way: "Once a single great passion occupies the soul, it displaces everything else. There is no room in us for two passions." Is not this Eden returned? Eden was a perfect garden as long as Adam had a single God. It was when he divided his affection between God and the snake that his perfect relationship was transformed to twisted worship.

Jesus affirmed this single focus when he said, "If anyone would come after me, he must deny himself and take up his cross daily and follow me" (Luke 9:23). Jesus was saying that all who call themselves his disciple must be possessed of a single passion for absolute obedience to him. No deviation—no disqualifying affection for other values, no place for other Lords!

Yet I know I must never allow this single focus to force me into narrowness. I cannot tell you why, but when I am totally alone with Jesus I am most in touch with all things. The world of art and literature and, above all, nature is instantly opened unto me the moment that I enter my closet of prayer and there find myself alone with Christ.

How far does Jesus carry his demand that I be possessed by a single driving passion? "If anyone comes to me and does not hate his father and mother, his wife and children, his brothers and sisters—yes, even his own life—he cannot be my disciple" (Luke 14:26). Was Jesus actually condoning family abandonment or a disregard for a solid home? Of course not. But he was saying, "Singleness of passion is right." To split our focused souls between two passions is sin. Small wonder Kierkegaard said, "Purity of heart is to will one thing." Wanting two things at once splits the soul. Wanting two things at once is sin. The more opposite these two things are, the worse the sin.

For sure our sins weigh us down. Author Madeleine L'Engle wrote of the burden of it all more than thirty years ago in a poem called *Ascension 1969*:

Pride is heavy.
It weighs.
It is a fatness of spirit,
An overindulgence in self.
This gluttony is earthbound
Cannot be lifted up.
Help me to fast,

To lose weight!
Otherwise, O Light One,
How can I rejoice in your ascension?[4]

Pride is indeed a fat and heavy sin. It too wants two things at once. It adores God even as it worships itself. It is an obesity of ego. When I am swollen with my own self-importance, I rarely turn to God. "I love me" is a great barrier to full intimacy with my Father.

When asked what the greatest commandment was, Jesus said, "Love the Lord your God with all your heart . . . Love your neighbor as yourself" (Mark 12:30–31). So I can never master my sin by sitting around with a pious look, crying repeatedly, "I will not sin, I will not sin, I will not sin!" This negative preoccupation with not sinning leads us ever toward the distinct probability we will.

A friend of mine once taught his daughter how to ride a bicycle. The place he chose for those unforgettable lessons was a wide, black-topped parking lot. While it had been striped for diagonal parking, there was not a single vertical obstruction anywhere in the lot except for a single pole located near the far edge of the lot. His instructions to his daughter were, "Be careful; don't hit the pole." There were acres of asphalt and only one twelve-inch pole. But it seemed to my friend that his daughter managed to direct her frenzied peddling directly into destruction. She could not have hit the pole more precisely if it had been her only life goal.

It seems there is a direct correlation between hearing "Don't do this or that" and the assurance we will do this or that. To say, "Don't get drunk" only causes the potential drunkard to spend the rest of the day thinking about bars.

But again, isn't the alcoholic's burden the sin of wanting two very different things at the same time? Of choosing both freedom and indulgence at once? Jean Pierre De Caussade wrote that our duty is obedience to God and the single worship that it inspires. He warned against the sin of trying to live any other way:

> You are trying to discover the secret of how to belong to God . . . Everything leads to union with him; everything brings about perfection excepting sin and what is not our duty. Only take things as they come without interfering. Everything guides, purifies and sustains you, carrying you along, so to speak, under God's banner, by whose hand earth, air and water are made divine.[5]

What a powerful notion this is, that those who are single in their passion for loving God have by a single passion sanctified the world around them. When we eliminate our double passion, the entire world falls into oneness. Eden has again returned. When his mind is our mind, we have but one mind between the two of us. Then we can walk together in the cool of the day with our Lord.

Sin is essentially egoistic and morality is essentially self-denial. The beginning of all sin is rooted in self-serving. In essence the motto of all sin is "If it feels good, do it!" and the anthem of all sinners is probably the anonymous little jingle:

> *I love meself, I love meself,*
> *I pick me up, and hug meself,*
> *I put me arm around me waist*
> *And get so fresh, I slap me face.*

Henrik Ibsen said the same sin that produces self-love ultimately produces self-absorption. Self-absorption, he said, ultimately produces mental illness. Mental illness at last fills mental institutions with the mentally ill, but each step along the way is a case of self-absorption of some sort. Ibsen may have overstated it, and he cannot be expected to have spoken for all mental illness, for there are forms of it that are wholly clinical and other forms that result from immense stress not related to inordinate self-love. But let's hear him out to this extent: he thought mental illness to be an extreme case of self-absorption. He believed asylums were places where each person shut the soul off in a cask of self, stopped with the bung of self and seasoned in a well of self. The destructive quality that sets paranoid people apart is a continual absorbtion of self.

THE SAVAGE SELF

The ultimate end of all self-serving is the abuse of power and the desire to control others—which we arrive at through self-love. When human beings over-love themselves they become a terror to their world and bind the planet in wounds and injuries. Such humans are not *Homo sapiens,* "man the knowing," but *Homo ferox,* "man the savage," said author T. H. White.

There is not a humble animal that does not flee from the shadow of man, as a burnt soul from purgatory. Not a mammal, not a fish, not a bird. Extend your walk so that it passes by a river bank, and the very fish will dart away . . . There is not a tiger, not a cobra, not an elephant in the African jungle, but what he flies from man . . .

Homo Ferox . . . that rarity in nature . . . which will kill for leisure . . . the sheep with its intelligent and sensitive face . . . kept solely in order to be slaughtered on the verge of maturity and devoured by their carnivorous herder . . . read about baking moles alive . . . *Homo Ferox* . . . who will rear pheasants at enormous expense for the pleasure of killing them . . . who will go to the trouble of training other animals to kill . . . who will burn living rats . . . in order that their shrieks may intimidate the local rodents; who will forcibly degenerate the livers of domestic geese in order to make himself a tasty food . . . who will saw the growing horns off cattle for convenience in transport; who will blind goldfinches with a needle to make them sing, who will boil lobsters and shrimps alive, although he hears their piping screams. Who will turn on his own species in war and will kill nineteen million every hundred years . . .[6]

For my own part, the greatest of all sins are interpersonal. I grew up in fundamentalist Oklahoma. I was told again and again there were certain sins that God despised. These were generally known in our congregation as the Big Five: playing cards, dancing, drinking, movies, and smoking. These were the sins most commonly preached on. There were lesser sins such as flamboyant makeup, jewelry, dipping snuff, short skirts, and the like. Every revivalist denounced these sins and told us how God hated them, yet never cited a scriptural reference. They were usually pointed out as sins against our bodies, which were the temples of the Holy Spirit. That *was* in the Bible, said the evangelist.

While I heard these things preached often in the 1940s, I never heard racism or genocide denounced a single time in my childhood. Yet the entire world at that very time was sweltering under Nazism and Fascism.

It took me years of maturity to grow to the place where I could see that the worst sins were those directed against either the dignity or survival of other peoples. Nazism defined the horror of those immense sins our revivalists never mentioned.

To label any race as inferior or worthy of being eradicated must be the greatest evil to confront the heart of God. I wondered during the trials of Nazi Adolf Eichmann how he had ever become so guilty of those horrors over which he had officiated.

But somewhere Eichmann had sinned the big sin— the people-sin. He made a godless decision that some people weren't really "people" when compared to other kinds of people. Some say it happened at one of those mass graves where Jews were put in the graves alive, shot, and then buried by bulldozers. The story is that as he officiated at one such horrible execution, one mother from the trench cried out, "Shoot me, but please take my baby." They say that Eichmann at first reached to take the child she extended upward to him, then he turned, stiffened his spine, and walked away. The first rifle shot caught the baby and the second folded the mother and her child together in death. The bulldozers rolled on and the next six million people were but paperwork for his regime.

One can easily study Eichmann and feel a kind of truth in the bumper sticker, "Hurt no one, and do what you please." If Eichmann had been willing to put that bumper sticker on his car and live it from his heart, the horror of the Holocaust might have been averted.

God has arranged in Christ that all our atrocities can be forgiven when we find real absolution in the blood of our Savior. The worst of sin does not merely hurt others, it depersonalizes them until they are no longer real people with the same hurts and needs as we have.

Of course, most of us will never be guilty of the high crimes of Auschwitz, Selma, or Oklahoma City. But unfortunately, we are ofttimes guilty of seeing our own denomination as superior. As a child I remember how often we Baptists vilified Methodists for being liberal. We heard they doubted the Bible, played down the resurrection, and scoffed at the virgin birth. I was years beyond my childhood before I found out that all these charges were false. But in the meantime my childhood Baptist prejudices reigned supreme.

I can remember as an adolescent, smoking a cigarette behind the grocery store. The store was called Simmon's Grocery. There was a common joke around our high school which begged the question, "Do you know where bad boys go for smoking?" The answer was, "Yes, behind Simmon's Grocery." I remember feeling very bad that I had participated in the evil of going there to smoke. Yet I must confess that these kinds of sins never made me feel as bad as when I actually wounded someone else. Each time I acted out a prejudice, I knew I hurt God more than those times in which I only fractured some Baptist taboo.

Jesus recognized that his people resented Samaritans and justified their prejudices with religious arguments. There were likely any number of ethnic jokes circulated that made sport of Samaritans. So Jesus told the story of the Good Samaritan to rip into these widespread prejudices. Those who shared these prejudices must have been utterly amazed to hear Jesus making a

Samaritan the hero of his story. It would be much like a fundamentalist pastor telling his people the story of the Good Homosexual or the Good Abortionist. Unable to separate the sin from the sinner, so often we label those we don't care for as much less loved of God than the Bible proclaims them to be.

The sin of dehumanizing others begins in the little game of *Us and Them*. Who has not played it? The game always sees *us* as a little more noble than *them*. I find this is a particularly fashionable game among church factions. *Us* is usually the conservative Bible believers— we are special to God because we take our stand and we honor his Word. We are unlike *them*—those people who are liberal and who doubt. In my early years as a Christian *they* always wore makeup and jewelry and smoked and read new translations of the Bible. In my later years, *they* held to belief in the social gospel or gave too little to missions or failed to censure presidential immorality.

The game of *Us and Them* comes to be because we are always on the lookout for people like ourselves. Such people have the "right ideas"—they think the way we do. They have our views on morality, our views on how one should be baptized or how we should feel about race or sexuality or the Bible. We spend very little of our time cultivating friendships with people who are different from us and who might broaden our worldview with new ideas. Instead we cultivate relationships with those who are so like us we can snuggle down into the warm theologies of our common nest.

CONCLUSION

The game of *Us and Them* begins the very moment you remove heaven's spectacles and lose track of how God views other people. The moment I take the God-view, I instantly reduce my own specialness to God.

I was in Agra, India, standing alone at the train platform waiting for the Taj Express to take me back to Delhi. The weather was hot and I had bought myself a small four-ounce paper cup of strawberry ice cream in an attempt to endure the sweltering heat. No sooner had I opened the cup of ice cream than I became aware of a sea of eyes—children, small, dirty, and hungry, looking up at me. I had quickly labeled them "small, dirty, and hungry" to feel my own advantage in being "big, clean, and well fed."

But I suddenly took the God-view. I instantly realized we were not all that different. I had been privileged to be born in a country where my circumstances permitted me to travel in theirs. Most of them would live and die within a few miles of where they had been born. But God loved us equally and our needs for approval, food, and self-esteem were not different.

I took the small treat and handed it to a little child with overlarge eyes. As he reached to take it, a sea of small brown arms reached to intercept the dessert. I don't know why I did it, but I stepped between the intended child and the flood of interceptors. I gave the boy the ice cream just before he leapt into his mother's filthy sari, where he began to devour this sticky-sweet delicacy. He looked at me with thankful approval as the rest of the world fell away. Our eyes met. We were one. We were both children of God. I could no longer dehumanize him and it never occurred to him to dehumanize me.

"He will wash away my sin," runs the song. "Let His little child come in." At the end of each day, I ask God to forgive my sins. This is a habit I formed years ago in childhood. I trust I will never lay it aside. But always at the top of my list are the sins I have committed against people.

These sins are the ones that most offend heaven. These offenses always presume that God doesn't care about the people I disdain. If ever I quit committing this sin, all my other sins will dwindle to such insignificance, the kingdom of God will be born instantly. Heaven and earth will be so united as to be indistinguishable.

Questions for Reflection

1. How do you feel about using the following epigram to define sin: "Hurt no one, and do what you please."

2. Paraphrase this statement: "If anyone says 'I love God,' yet hates his brother, he is a liar."

3. Paraphrase this statement: "God will not tolerate my serving two gods at once. Every polygamy of the heart is regarded as idolatry in heaven."

4. What did Kierkegaard mean when he wrote, "Purity of heart is to will one thing"?

5. Why does the author say, "Wanting two things at once is sin"?

6. Do you agree with this statement: "The basis of most of our sin really lies in the desire to feel good somehow." Why or why not?

7. Do you feel that the following statement is true: "The ultimate end of all self-serving is the abuse of power and the desire to control others."

8. How does faith in Christ effect T. H. White's assumption that human beings are not *Homo sapien* ("man the knowing") but *Homo ferox* ("man the savage")? Is the person who will not know the taming love of Christ more prone to brutalize the world with savage power? Why do you think so? Why would you never think so?

9. Do you agree with this: "To label any race as inferior or worthy of being hated or eradicated [by genocide] must be the sins of greatest evil to the heart of God." What can believers do to seek to promote a respect for all people? What can we do to help others eradicate their prejudices?

10. What does the following statement mean: "The sin of dehumanizing others begins in the little game of *Us and Them.*"

11. Paraphrase this so that a small child could read and understand it: "The sins that matter most presume that God doesn't care about what we don't care about."

CHAPTER 10

He Will Stay Close Beside Me All the Way

Dear Friend:

How are you? I just had to send you this letter and to tell you how much I love and care about you. I saw you yesterday as you were walking with friends. I waited all day hoping you would talk to me also. As evening drew near, I gave you a sunset to close your day, a cool breeze to rest you, and I waited. You never came. Oh, yes, it hurt me, but I still love you, because I am your friend.

I saw you fall asleep last night, and I longed to touch your brow, so I spilled moonlight upon your pillow and face. Again I waited, wanting to rush down so we could talk. I have so many gifts for you.

You awakened late and rushed off for the day—my tears were in the rain. Today you looked so sad, so alone. It makes my heart ache because I understand. My friends let me down and hurt me many times, too, but I love you. I try to tell you in the quiet, green grass. I whisper it in the leaves and the trees, and give it in the color of the flowers. I shout it to you in the mountain streams, and give the birds love songs to sing. I clothe you with warm sunshine and perfume the air. My love for you is deeper than the oceans, and bigger than the biggest want or need you have.

We will spend eternity together in heaven. I know how hard it is on this earth, I really know . . . My father wants to help you too . . . He's that way, you know. Just call on me, ask me, talk to me . . . But if you don't call, you'll see . . . I have chosen you and because of this, I will wait . . . because I love you.

Your friend,

Jesus

AUTHOR UNKNOWN

A CONVERSATION WITH JESUS

Lord, what I crave more than all else is the promise of your presence.

This you have. I will never leave you nor forsake you. But I would not have your craving appear as though it were unique to you. Do you really long to be with me? Do you ache for our togetherness? Then know this: all you desire is doubled in my craving. I long equally to be with you.

But what about those times when the way is hard? Can I count on you then?

Yea, though you walk through the valley of the shadow of death, you need not fear. I will be with you—a table of peace in the presence of your ene-mies. When your world is complicated by those who cannot stand to have you near and would raise their own self-importance to harm you, I call you to my table. There you will sample my peace. Your presence will be my joy—your enemies will not matter.

But when the assault of Satan falls on me like hail on tender crops—can I know, really know, you are with me, then?

Even then I will keep you as the apple of my eye—I will hide you beneath the shadow of my wings.

I will gather you under my wings as a hen gathers her brood of chicks. You have but to travel with me— Follow me for I have prepared a place for you.

But Lord how can I know which way is the way you go?

Follow me, I am the Way, the Truth and the Life. There is only one road—I am that way. To travel any other is to deceive yourself that there are other ways to other destinations. I am the journey. The entire journey. I am your embarkation, your destiny! I am your final altar at the gates of God's foreverness.

Then I can always depend on your nearness?

Lo, I am always with you. If you rise to the heavens I will be there. If you make your bed in the depths I will be there. If you rise on the wings of the dawn and make your bed on the far side of the sea I will be there. Lo, I will be with you always even to the end of the world. And when this world ends, the causeway you have traveled will open on our bright, unending oneness.

HEBREWS 13:5; PSALM 23:4–5; PSALM 17:8; LUKE 13:34; JOHN 14:4; JOHN 14:6; PSALM 139:7–9; MATTHEW 28:20

Loneliness is the work of a single demon known as separation. We call ourselves "lonely" and in pronouncing the word concur that we are separated from all who care about us. Being alone sponsors the feeling that might be confronted by enemies too strong for us. We feel we have nowhere to turn for protection. The worst of all prison terrors is solitary confinement. What is so horrible about being shut in a room entirely by ourselves with no one to talk to? This aloneness speaks to our worst fear—the fear of meeting the great unmanageable dread—ourselves. So "Jesus loves me! He will stay close beside me all the way" is God's answer to the terror of aloneness.

This terror compounds itself when we suspect we may actually be in danger. To be alone and under any threat magnifies our inner terror. When I was a child in the early forties, I had an odd addiction to horror films. The technology of 1940s monster films was not well developed by today's standard. The special effects were not so special. Still, they were quite enough to terrify me. I particularly liked and feared Lon Chaney, who looked something like a Baptist deacon I once knew who had terrified me as a child. But in those black-and-white thrillers the actor changed into a wolf-man. And he not only made me miserable while I watched the movie, he stalked me all the way home from the theater.

I specifically remember a grove of locust trees only a

block or two from my home. If the moon was full I feared to pass that thicket. I could see this deacon look-alike fiend as he grew fur and fangs and stalked my loneliness. I whistled hymns as I passed that terrifying grove—at least till I ran out of spit. When my mouth was too dry to whistle, I ran all the way home as fast as I could. The imagined monster seemed too near to escape. The hot breath of the fiend was close at hand, but in three short leaps I cleared the front steps of our home and found my mother even closer at hand. In her presence the terror disappeared. I was free. Presence is the great reply to terrifying aloneness. It lies at the heart of Christ's promise that he will stay close beside me all the way.

As I grew older I came to see that Christ's nearness was the cure for my fears. He defangs werewolves and exorcises the demons that make me tremble.

Was my fear valid? Of course not. Enid, Oklahoma, is a long way from Transylvania. Not a single wolf—"were" or more traditional—has ever been captured near Enid. A "were-coyote" would have been a more reasonable fiction. Still, the fiends that rise from a child's imagination are real enough to terrorize a child.

There are more reasonable bogeymen in my current life.

Recently I've seen the monsters that haunt the aged. I've seen the ravaged elderly staring vacantly into the Lysol atmosphere of state-managed nursing homes. No one ever comes to see these vacant souls. They merely tremble at first, and later they become empty, hopeless, human masks—dry souls waiting each day for someone—anyone—to come and end their isolation from the world.

And I've heard children's workers in day-care programs tell of little ones whose parents drop them off early in the morning—before dawn. Some children rock back and forth, hour after hour, talking to no one. They sadly enforce their own loneliness until the end of the day when, for the first time, they squeal with delight because their parents have come to end their long, long vigil of desperation.

Paul lamented his lonely imprisonment: "At my first answer," he confessed, "no one stood with me. Yet the Lord stood with me" (see 2 Tim. 4:16–17). This is the exact sentiment of the children's hymn. This is the promise of his presence. Jesus loves me; he will stay close beside me all the way.

Our day is one in which cities are crowded but people live pretty much alone. It is a day in which multitudes are living in the midst of the lonely crowds. But the presence of Jesus comes like a warm spring rain to end the arid loneliness. A hymnwriter wrote: "I come to the Garden alone, while the dew is still on the roses."[1] Some suggest this beautiful hymn was written by a sewer attendant in an Asian prison who was condemned to shovel human excrement all his life. Yet by his own will he sanctified his sea of sewage, transforming it into a garden where the presence of Christ changed his unthinkable loneliness to a quiet talk with his best friend in a garden.

Forty years ago, when I was a student in a Kansas City seminary, the body of a young girl was fished out of the Missouri River not far from our home. On her faded blouse was pinned a water-streaked note that read: "I haven't a friend in the world. Nobody cares about me."

Loneliness is a killer.

At the same time the city newspaper ran an article about an "old-folks home" where an aged, dying resident left behind a journal that read on page after page,

"No one came today . . . No one came today . . . No one came today."

Loneliness is a killer.

Our society is afflicted with a viral loneliness. It has become so customary that most of the lonely have learned to insulate themselves against the pain of it all with overloud music and manic schedules. They will do anything to not feel alone. One of the plaintive cries I recall from my years as a pastor was from a ninety-year-old woman who, having outlived her children and grandchildren, pleaded, "Pastor, please stay with me till I 'cross over.' I have no one else to be with me when I die, and I've always feared dying all by myself. I have no fear of dying, I just never wanted to be alone when I did it."

A PRESENCE IN LONELINESS

Much has been conquered by those who found purpose in their loneliness. When I first read *One Day in the Life of Ivan Denisovich*, I felt it was in some ways the most powerful novel I had ever read. It was only later that I learned it had been derived directly from Solzhenitsyn's solitary imprisonment. Knowing that he dared not be caught writing a state-unapproved book, he wrote the novel in short paragraphs, which he committed to memory before destroying the paper. When he had finished his lonely confinement, he was released from the prison and then wrote down the entire work from memory.

Solitude is one of the spiritual disciplines. It is always the hardest. Some spend their solitude praying or reading the Bible. But to voluntarily shut ourselves away from our world of conversation and commerce is indeed hard.

Some monks, on entering their orders, take a vow of silence. They enter into such a vow because they realize there is a kind of death in human chattiness. They also know that it is when we quit talking that we begin listening. Solitude gives God a mouth by making us an ear. Frankly, the best way to hear from God is to shut up. In the resulting silence we can hear the strains of "Jesus loves me! He will stay close beside me all the way." It is God's whisper to our togetherness with Christ.

Jesus taught us by example that his own togetherness with God was made possible by withdrawing from his friends. What worlds he breached—what worlds he conquered with solitude. If his "seven last words" do indeed represent all he said during the ordeal of the cross, he remained relatively quiet. Yet in this solitude he won eternity for the human race. Isaiah said of Jesus that he was led as a "lamb to the slaughter, and as a sheep before her shearers is dumb, so he openeth not his mouth" (Isa. 53:7 KJV). How dark and fearsome was the solitude he endured to join the realms of heaven and earth.

Charles Lindberg, in some ways, seems a grand metaphor of Jesus. He took off on his 1926 flight and without landing lights flew over the Atlantic, cutting through the dark skies. I have made the same trip many times now on huge jets. My flights are passed in comfort and ease, but how much I owe a man who lived in loneliness to pave the way. When Lindberg landed in France, the Parisians who owned cars went down to the airfield and shined their lights on the unpaved runway to point the final way for his landing. Because of the hours of the solitude this man took upon himself, America and Europe enjoyed a new kind of togetherness. For this feat Lindberg earned the title of "Lone Eagle." I routinely pay tribute to the Lone Eagle.

This is not so different from how I feel about Jesus. He conquered death by going through it first. In the Book of Hebrews the writer referred to Jesus as the *archegos*, the pioneer—the "first goer" (see Heb. 12:2). He was the Lone Eagle of Eternity, and one day I shall easily soar the path he showed me how to fly by going there first.

In a similar way I'm bound for heaven and yet how easy he has made it.

He who died is
He who will stay
Close beside me all the way.

Perhaps Ben Gunn, the isolated wild-man in Robert Louis Stevenson's *Treasure Island*, provides the model for all that loneliness requires. Remember the plaintive and pitiful model of all he displayed? He was half-mad and full of quaint and odd quirks from his years of isolation.

I once knew an old man whose children had abandoned him years earlier. Like Ben Gunn, he lived alone and bemoaned his empty room and vacuous life. He loved poetry—particularly Kipling—and with a vacant eye would stare into space quoting the verses as far away from the rest of the world as though he himself were marooned in a wild and lofty Tibetan temple.

The wild craving of all such lonely desperate people is presence. The child's hymn wakes the presence of Jesus, who "will stay close beside me all the way." Yes, amen! All the way? Yes, all the way. This is a promise of presence indeed, and so in concert with the rest of the Bible.

- Lo, I am with you always [said Jesus]. (Matt. 28:20 KJV)
- God is our refuge and strength, a very present help in trouble. (Ps. 46:1 KJV)
- I will fear no evil: for thou art with me. (Ps. 23:4)
- Have not I commanded thee? . . . Be not afraid, neither be thou dismayed: for the LORD thy God is with thee whithersoever thou goest. (Jos. 1:9 KJV)
- I will never leave you nor forsake you. (Heb. 13:5)

The most appealing thing about Jesus is the promise of his presence.

DEPENDING ON THE PRESENCE

The child of wealthy parents in our church was once kidnapped only a few blocks from her home. Her abductors blindfolded the little girl, drove her miles away, and hid her in an old shed. Several times they threatened her, promising to take her life. But each time she told them that Jesus was stronger than they were and he had no intention of letting them hurt her. Within two days their threats began to dissipate and they finally let her out at a nearby convenient store. She was unharmed.

Children often possess an uncanny ability to feel this presence as an unforsaking protector. They seem to believe what they sing: He really will be with us "all the way."

In 1954 the Supreme Court ordered America's schools to desegregate and in 1960 the Frantz school in New Orleans complied. Robert Coles won the Pulitzer Prize for his dramatic work with children. He was outside the building on the day of the federally mandated integration of the Frantz school. One of the children who endeared herself to Coles that day was Ruby Bridges. Ruby was a little girl who faced the barricades when the forced integration of the school system was occurring. It was a marvel to see this beautiful, little, African-American girl pass through the leering, ugly faces of white defiance and continue on into the school. One would think the charged atmosphere of racial hate would have driven the child into despair, but it did not.

When Coles and others asked Ruby how she had managed to pass the barricades with a smiling confidence, she simply said she prayed. She prayed and asked Jesus to be with her. He obviously was. Christ's presence in a child's life made the child as strong as steel—and an immense force for social justice.

It is believing children who best teach us the practice of the presence of God. He really will stay close beside us all the way. Robert Coles wrote this of what he saw:

> Outside the Frantz school I saw a mob of people standing and screaming. It was two o'clock in the afternoon, and I realized they were waiting for something. I asked one of the people what was happening.
>
> He answered, "She's coming out in a half an hour."
>
> I said, "Who's she?"
>
> And then I heard all the language about who she was—all the cuss words and the foul language. I decided to stay and watch, even if I didn't get to see my doctor.
>
> Soon, out of the Frantz school came a little girl, Ruby Bridges. And beside her were federal mar-

shals. She came out and the people started in. They called her this and they called her that. They brandished their fists. They told her she was going to die and they were going to kill her. I waited when she left in a car, and I wondered who was going to come out of the school next. But then I found out no one else was in the school. The school had been totally boycotted by the white population. So here was a little black child who was going to an American elementary school all by herself in the fall of 1960. This is part of our American history.[2]

With the aid of Kenneth Clark, a New England psychologist, Dr. Coles was later able to establish a relationship with the Bridges family. He asked Ruby's mother how the child was holding up under the pressure:

"How do you think Ruby's doing with her friends when she comes home from school?"

"Ruby's fine when she comes home. She plays and sometimes she reads from the books that she brings home, or tries to read the books. She's just in the first grade, learning how to read."

"Does Ruby seem upset at any time?"

"No, Ruby doesn't seem too upset," said Mrs. Bridges.

Mrs. Bridges told me Ruby had been told, in Sunday school, to pray for the people. I later found that the minister in their Baptist church also prayed for the people. Publicly. Every Sunday. . . .

"We're not asking her to pray for them because we want to hurt her or anything," said Mrs. Bridges, "but we think that we all have to pray for people like that, and we think Ruby should too."[3]

One cannot fail to be impressed that the prayer that Ruby found so available imparted to her a deep sense of the abiding presence of Christ.

The presence of Jesus is a most important promise to the despairing. The psalmist sang, "Though I walk through the valley of the shadow of death, I will fear no evil: for thou art with me, thy rod and thy staff they comfort me" (Ps. 23:4 KJV). His presence in the valley is where we seek and find the comfort necessary to our existence.

But a child's confidence about the constant accompaniment of Christ gives way at last to our adult confidence that Christ is with us. I think of the Celtic statement called "The Breastplate of St. Patrick":

> *Christ to protect me to-day*
> *against poison, against burning,*
> *against drowning, against wounding,*
> *so that there may come abundance of reward.*
> *Christ with me, Christ before me, Christ behind me,*
> *Christ in me, Christ beneath me, Christ above me,*
> *Christ on my right, Christ on my left,*
> *Christ where I lie, Christ where I sit, Christ where I arise,*
> *Christ in the heart of every man who thinks of me,*
> *Christ in the mouth of every man who speaks of me,*
> *Christ in every eye that sees me,*
> *Christ in every ear that hears me.*

There is no single joy quite like that of knowing we are not alone in facing our worst fears.

PRACTICING THE PRESENCE

One of the most meaningful classics on Jesus is Brother Lawrence's *Practicing the Presence of God*. Brother Lawrence—as I said earlier—was a cook in a monastery. It fell his lot to spend about all of his adult life in the kitchen—usually up to his elbows in dishwater. Brother Lawrence learned that if ever he got to know God he was going to have to make the kitchen his cathedral and a sink full of dirty dishes his altar. So while he scrubbed and scoured, he got to know God. And his dishwater baptized the world with insight on how to live continually in the never-failing presence of Christ.

But the nearness of Christ is often granted first to those whose need mandates that presence. Jesus draws near the needy precisely because the self-sufficient seem to have all the company they crave. I have a friend who is severely challenged with cerebral palsy and who is now in her mid-forties. She told me one day that more than anything she wanted to have a home, a husband, and children. But the swift decades and her misshapen, spastic movements relegated her to lonely intervals of existence. She confessed to me in an aching conversation, "All my life I have prayed for a home—I know I would make a good wife, and a good mother. But who would marry me?" She spoke further, "Do you know what bothers me the most? Not in all these years has anyone seen me as pretty."

I felt convicted in my heart. I had to confess inwardly that I saw her as spiritually brave, beautiful, and courageous. Yet inwardly every woman—every man—at least once in life wants to be seen as attractive. She knew, and I could see, she would likely never marry. For me it was one of those "what a shame" moments, but for her it was the preoccupation of a lifetime.

"Still," she said, "the bright thing about my future is what remains the bright thing about each day: Jesus will never be an incidental luxury for me. I must have him or there is no sunrise and old age is impossible."

Never till I had this conversation did I understand that everything is usable to God. Jesus really loves me, he really will stay close beside me all the way. It was at this point that I thought of the faithfulness of God and something that John of the Cross once said. "Never pray for friends," he said. "Pray only that you may have enemies, for only when you have enemies will you retreat of necessity to the Savior." Obviously the best cure for human loneliness is the Savior himself; there is no other cure but Jesus. The best promise of his presence is realized not just when Jesus is at hand but when he is the only one with us.

JESUS' PRESENCE IN THE HARD PLACES

It is Jesus' presence in the hard places of life that convince us he is the no-quit Savior. Abraham Lincoln was reported to have said, "I have been driven to my knees many times on the overwhelming conviction I had nowhere else to go." At such moments we burst again into the children's anthem, "Jesus loves me! He will stay close beside me all the way."

In the dark moments of isolation when I hear no one speaking to me and it is clear I am altogether alone, I still sense Jesus in the shadows. Thomas à Kempis observed:

> Blessed is that man who hears Jesus speaking in his soul . . . Blessed are those ears which hear the secret whisperings of Jesus . . . Thus says your beloved: I am our health, I am your peace, I am your life. Keep yourself in me and you will find peace in me . . . What help can any creature be to you if your Lord Jesus forsake you?[4]

We thrill to feel his presence in the hard places.

I like contrasting Mary, the mother of the teenage Jesus, with Mary, the mother of the crucified Jesus. Consider Mary when Jesus was twelve years old and she had lost him in the temple. Upon leaving Jerusalem Mary and Joseph had been on the road for a day before they realized they had not seen Jesus in a while; then they sought for him among their relatives. Not finding him, they hurried back into the city and looked for three more days. They at last found him among the doctors in the temple. How did Mary ever lose track of Jesus like this?

At the crucifixion, Jesus was dying on the cross above her, and she could not lose track of where he was. Why? Because her own soul was destroyed by all she suffered as she saw Christ die. She lost him on the road because she was doubtless involved with the good times and laughter of her pilgrimage. Jesus was in no danger and she wasn't either. She was enjoying her family, the sun was shining, and the presence of her son wasn't nearly as important to her own well-being. But by the end of Luke she was broken by the ugly circumstances of existence. Now she is in the valley of the shadow. Then she was transfixed by the power of his love. Mary knew a oneness she could never have known when she needed Jesus less.

What a metaphor she provides for our own lives.

In the hassle of our empty hurriedness we often ask, "Are you running with me, Jesus?" It's a fair question but usually needless. Jesus rarely runs with us. So the next time you find yourself devoted to the religious hassle, you may be sure that Jesus is more your Messiah at a slower, thoughtful pace.

Walk and the Lord will walk with you, run and you may run alone! For the Christ of the hard places convinces you of his presence at a slow pace. There, between stops, you can look into his eyes, and your hand knows the grip of something wounded. And you will feel his blood intermingled with your own. Christ did not hurry to redeem you over his lunch hour and he will not give you heaven's counsel while you offer him your coffee breaks and withhold your reflective hours.

His presence in the valley is proof of how far he will walk at the pace of your suffering. Indeed, happy are they who remember that oftentimes the pain comes so we can see that he is present with us. Author Laura A. Barter Snow wrote:

> My child, I have a message for you today; let me whisper it in your ear, that it may gild with glory any storm clouds that may arise, and smooth the rough places on which you have to tread. It is short, only five words, but let them sink into your inmost soul; use them as a pillow upon which to rest your weary head: "*This thing is from me.*" . . . Are you passing through a night of sorrow? This thing is from me. I am the "Man of sorrows and acquainted with grief." I have let earthly comforters fail you, that by

turning to me you may obtain everlasting consolation (2 Thess. 2:16–17) . . . I could not get your attention in your busy days and I want to teach you some of my deepest lessons . . . The sting will go as you learn to see me in all things.[5]

How true it is that we often feel the presence of Jesus and the presence of trouble at the same time. Generally the trouble comes slightly ahead of his presence. The trouble creates the need and his presence ends our self-sufficiency. Then the Lord who has been with us all along suddenly makes himself known. He never leaves us in our times of self-sufficiency, and he never declares himself when we are confident we can handle things on our own.

I can never get over the fable of Mandy and Lisa. Lisa had lost a child and her need for the presence of God soared. At last, because God seemed too absent in her time of need, she went to see her best friend, Mandy. "Oh, Mandy," she said, "I've cried out to God and he is not there!"

"Oh, Lisa, sometimes it seems that way, but when I pray and can't find God, I just ask him to come out of his hiding place and lay his hand on my shoulder."

"And does he do it?"

"Of course he does, Lisa. Just try it. You'll see!"

Immediately Lisa clamped her eyes shut and began to pray. "God, this is Lisa. If you're really there in my time of need, I want you to come out of your hiding place and lay your hand on my shoulder so I'll know you care."

As she prayed, Mandy slipped up behind her and laid her hand on Lisa's shoulder.

Lisa finished her prayer, turned, faced her old friend, and cried, "Oh Mandy, it's true! All true! It's just as you said. I asked God, if he was really there, to lay his hand on my shoulder and he did it! He did it! He laid his hand on my shoulder. It felt just like your hand, Mandy."

"Shucks, Lisa, honey, it was Mandy's hand. While you were praying, the Lord spoke to me and said, 'Mandy, honey, my little friend Lisa is in a heap of hurt. Why don't you slip up behind her and put your hand on her shoulder, just so she'll never forget I'm right there with her in her times of trouble.'"

So often, finding the presence of God is being with someone who has a keener spiritual eye than we do. Sometimes the troubles we feel cause us to need Jesus and then we can clearly see him. At other times our troubles are so terrible we find they obscure the presence of Christ rather than point it out.

In *The Silence of God,* author Helmut Theilicke said that when the bombs were falling on his parish in Stuttgart in World War II, he would often hear people in the bomb shelters praying in one of two ways. They would either be praying, *"Lord,* save us from the bombs," or they would be praying, "Lord, save us from the *bombs."* In the former prayer, the needy were usually focused on the presence of God and the bombs held no sway over their ability to see God. But in the latter prayer, those would be seeking to find the presence of God while they focused on the horror of bombs. They were trying to find God, but even as they did this their minds pictured not the serenity of God but missiles of destruction falling in fire and rubble on their lost fortunes.

It is then that Mandy and Lisa offer us the best view of healing. Is Jesus really there? Does he stay right beside us all the way?

I can remember several times as a pastor in which someone who faced the specter of death would cry out, "Where is God?" These cries do not label people as lifetime agnostics. They are but brief sallies into the despair of a darkened heart. Whenever I run into such despair, I always remind the needy one that God is not immune to hurt. He hurts when we do. He cries when we cry.

Let us remember that the whole idea of the Incarnation was that God became a man because it was the only way God could acquire a nervous system. As I earlier wrote, the Scriptures record when Jesus cried because he hurt. Who among us is glad that Jesus died such a painful death as he did? None! But had he slipped in and out of the planet without pain, how would he ever have understood ours? His death makes him our finest counselor when we face our own. Give me as my savior no Greek god who frolics in indulgence, gluttony, and adultery. Give me instead a God who can hang in suffocating pain and tell me, even as he gasps, that life is never pointless.

The question "Where is God?" has only one answer. "There he is! Upon the cross! Can't you see, he was dying before you were ever born into your particular world of trouble? You don't like crosses? Neither did he. You find the iron spikes gash your hands? So did he. You find yourself unable to think of a simple person who will stand with you? So did he."

But in the cross Jesus not only said, "Lo, I am with you always." What he really said was, "Lo, I am with you regardless!"

CONCLUSION

It is both his presence and difficulty that create the life beautiful. His presence without difficulty only creates the life superficial. The difficulty without his presence only creates a cynical life.

Perhaps it is hackneyed, but if the oyster could make pearls without difficulty, it doubtless would do so. And if the difficulty came to it without any hope of producing beauty, it would be a pointless hurt. Such oysters would reckon suicide to be meaningful. But in the difficulty lies the glory.

Every oyster must be honest. The sharp piece of stone is there. It is lodged in the center of life and cannot be moved. There is no way to turn without the pain. Then there is nothing to do but let the pain be. A drop of white ointment comes and bathes the knifing silicate. It is no use. The pain survives. Another drop comes, it anoints the wound, wrapping a mucous cushion all around the horror. The pain? Still there? Yes. On with life's secretions.

And then one day, the pain is gone! And where it was grows a gleam of light that would blind the court as it glistens in the crown of a great king.

Beauty has adorned the hurt and masked the treasure. Such is the birth of a pearl.

I once taught a class of widows in the church. I could not help but fall in love with them. What wondrous souls these widows were—gallant women whose lives beyond their husbands' deaths displayed the inner treasure God had fabricated from their hurt. They had tested the presence of God with pain, and their lives victoriously declared, "See, here is the pearl of his presence. Jesus loves us! He *will* stay close beside us all the way."

QUESTIONS FOR REFLECTION

1. Why do you think the worst of all prison terrors is solitary confinement? Why, in your opinion, is one of the worst terrors of our lives the terror of being alone? In what ways does conversation with other people tell us who we are and what our place is in the world?

2. Jesus seemed to have many times of self-imposed solitude. What did he do with the solitude he chose? How did he use it for purposes to seek his Father's will for his own life? How did He use it to enter into intercessory prayer for his disciples? Which of the two uses are of most use in the Christian's life?

3. How do think Ruby Bridges became so aware of God's participation in her life? How can we develop the same kind of confidence as adults? In what proportion do you find your fears shouting louder than your prayers and vice versa?

4. Brother Lawrence found that he had to learn to "practice the presence of God" in the kitchen if he were to learn to practice it at all. Mention five areas of your life where you find it impossible to stop, bow your head, and pray. How can you bring Christ into these hassled moments and find rest in his presence?

5. Can you think of one time when his presence and your dire circumstances created in you the "life beautiful"?

CHAPTER 11

If I Love Him When I Die,
He Will Take Me Home
on High

We shall hear a Voice of splendor echo through
    our halls,
Shake the portals of our being—
Separate the walls.
We shall hear a breathless Whisper creep across
    the air,
Mitigate our rasping edges,
Strip our fictions bare.
We shall hear a Song come sifting,
Shifting down from scale to scale,
Tuning earth to strings that shiver, timbres that
    impale.
We shall hear the Sound of heaven rumble over
    space,
Making room beyond the heavens
For His day of Grace.

JUDITH DEEM DUPREE[1]

A CONVERSATION WITH JESUS

Lord, what is life's most important work?

Love. There is no higher work—no harder work—
than love. It is exalted, for it is the greatest work of
God as well as the greatest work of human beings.
Love is hard, for it is sent to wash its enemies with
blessings while its enemies despise its coming. Still,
you shall love the Lord your God with all your heart
and with all your soul and with all your mind and
with all your strength.

*And what will be the result of my loving—will it be
giving. It has been said we can give without loving but we
cannot love without giving.*

It is true. Love defies its keeper never to be stingy.
Love drives all lovers to tell the world, "I am in
love—behold my ardor. Because I love, I give. I
cannot keep, I must relinquish what I own so none
may doubt my love."

*So I am to love you above all things, even above my
family?*

Love God first. Love him with all the love you
think you have, then you will discover you held a
great reserve for loving that you never knew you had.
Love me above all. If anyone comes to me and does

not hate his father and mother, his wife and children, his brothers and sisters—yes even his own life—he cannot be my disciple.

And if I truly love you how must I show it?

Serve. Put on your apron. Enter prisons and love the alienated. Enter orphanages and love the unadopted. Enter old-age homes and love the unremembered. In this way you will feed my lambs.

So love must serve, but how far must love go to do it?

How can I love people who so openly scorn or mistreat me?

Think you that I am a stranger to such abuse? I have wept over a whole city, crying my love while they readied their hammers for crucifixion. But the servant is not greater than his Lord, as I have loved you so you must love.

And what is the ultimate power of such loving?

If you love me you will do what I say. And obedience is the first trust of love. No one ever loved me who would not obey me. You can be my disciple only if you love others as I have loved you.

Mark 12:30; Luke 14:26; John 21:15;
John 2:15; 13:16; John 14:15; John 13:34–35

"If I love him when I die, He will take me home on high." What an odd line to stick in a children's song! Shall we take joyous little children, stuff them in pews, and force them to sing morosely of whom they will love when they die?

Believe it or not, children have a strange fascination with the idea of dying. Remember that the most famous of all "nighty-night" prayers offers this plea: "If I should die before I wake, I pray the Lord my soul to take." Where? Through those wide opened gates we find in verse two of "Jesus Loves Me."

As a child I could not help but be intrigued by that awful silence adults called death. When I was four years old, my ten-year-old brother died in a swimming accident. One of my earliest memories and most profound puzzles was the riddle of being lifted up over the edge of a very small coffin to see my silent brother for the final time. The overwhelming mystery of his stillness still haunts my childhood.

As a longtime pastor who has officiated at many funerals, I am still awed by the touching sight of little coffins. Yet in spending much time with children who struggle with terminal illnesses, I was always struck by the resignation with which a child faces the end. There is often an uncanny cheer about children. They seem to know they are dying but they take each uncertain day hour by hour, with more certainty and joy than I often find in adults. Most of those children I attended knew and loved Jesus and so were convinced that if they loved him when they died, he would take them home on high.

I visited one eight-year-old girl during her final days. She had been a national cystic-fibrosis poster child and had known almost movie-star adulation during her illness. Her chances to live were dependent on a heart-lung transplant that never came through. Each day the crucial transplant did not arrive was another day of dismal disappointment for her parents. Yet surprisingly, the little girl was never morose as she waited.

During her final days of life, she seemed to speak ever more confidently of being in heaven. There was no doubt in her mind that she was going there. And for her it seemed a welcome idea as her breathing became ever more difficult. She fought death one struggling gasp at a time. She seemed to anticipate heaven but clung to this life because she felt that leaving it would be a terrible grief to her parents.

I will never forget the anguish I sensed in her tiny, struggling frame. She seemed a living quotation of Philippians 1:23: "I am torn between the two: I desire to depart and be with Christ, which is better by far; but it is more necessary for you that I remain in the body." With all her might she clung to two worlds, refusing to let go of her grip on the here and now, even for the sake of the there and then.

Yet never have I seen dying children so eager for the next life that they refused to fight to stay biologically alive. More than most know, children plan to live a long time. They are not eager to abandon this life. In fact, most of what dying children picture when they talk of heaven, they phrase in terms of this life. One child, a cancer victim, spoke of heaven as being like a "house with many windows." Why such a metaphor? Who knows exactly, except perhaps that sick children spend a lot of time looking out of their windows. Illness is always a confinement, and the ill depend on windows to show them the real and better world outside. Eternal life too is a kind of window! It is a glimpse of the life beyond. Therefore heaven must be a house of many windows.

The finality of death does not always come with sharply defined edges.

Julian of Norwich, during a season of illness, was so near to death that those who attended her called in the priests to administer last rites. During this time, she, like Paul, seemed to have been "caught up to the third heaven" (2 Cor. 12:2). Then she experienced her famous "showings." Without a doubt this testament, *Showing of Love,* is the most profound spiritual classic in the English language. Dating from the era of Chaucer, it is one of the earliest pieces of Latin–English literature (and certainly the earliest written by a woman). But it is more than that—it is a testament of glory written by one who seemed to be "trapped" between worlds.

Malcolm Muggeridge confessed that his final years were lived on the cusp of heaven. He would wake up from a near escape, reaching for heaven but slammed hard back down to the earth. He wrote:

> You know, it's a funny thing that when you're very old, as I am, seventy-five and near dying, the queerest thing happens. You very often wake up about two or three in the morning and you are half in and half out of your body, a most peculiar situation. You can see your battered old carcass there between the sheets and it's quite a tossup

whether you resume full occupancy and go through another day or make off where you can see, like the lights in the sky as you're driving along, the lights of Augustine's *City of God*.[2]

The song "Jesus Loves Me" teaches us that he who loves me "will stay close beside me all the way." From infancy we, like Muggeridge, are always reckoning with finality. The odd metaphysics of dividing the soul from the still corpse we have decorated with flowers is hard to understand and almost impossible to explain to a child's complete satisfaction.

Miffy, one of the children in our church, died at five years of age. Having no idea why God called the little girl to heaven at such an early age, I found myself in a quandary as I prepared to officiate at her funeral. I preached to a rather large crowd of very bewildered people. It seemed in some ways they had purchased tickets to come to hear me explain a great riddle. Although I believed God held the ultimate resolution to the puzzle, I was as confused as they were.

The little girl's father was an adjutant to a general, so there were many high-level "brass" at the service. I think it was these "military mighty ones" that most befuddled me. They listened hard to my eulogy as if to say, "We're experts at war. Now we want to hear a word from a man who is an expert on death and dying." I am sure I was somewhat of a disappointment to them, for there are no experts on death and dying.

When I got through with the memorial service and the press of mourners had passed by the casket to pay their last respects to Miffy, I could think of little more to do than to hug them. But was it appropriate for a civilian to hug a general? With some reluctance I hugged . . . and with much exuberance they hugged back. Even for generals the best answer to the mystery of death was an embrace.

I offered this sonnet called "To Miffy" at the internment as the small white casket sank slowly into the ground:

I've waited till your second day. I knew
Your first day there would seem to you a treat.
You'd gaze about in wonder at the view
Of all that city gathered in one street.
So many I know here are quite afraid
To face their final fears and cross the sea.
You swam so easily! What courage made
You unafraid to walk eternity?

Did God appear a high-rise trinity?
Did glass or tow'ring crystal dazzle you?
Did he not cry, "Let this child come to me
And give her room to skip this avenue!"

At those grand gates which close against the night,
He scooped you up and carried you to light.

In some way it was easier for me to visualize a child skipping through heaven than to imagine some more grandiose heavenly images of angels armed with glass and thunderbolts.

Loving Jesus when we die is the rule—the porch of foreverness. Heaven is quite often a matter of theological speculation for those who have never lost children. But it is never so academic to those who have. Those who lose children can never be casual about heaven again. I observed this with my own mother who, following the death of my brother, spoke more avidly and fervently about the reality of heaven. His passing increased her certainty about eternity.

HEAVEN: THE HEART'S GREATEST LONGING

There is a strong relationship between innocence and holiness. The only difference between the two is that holiness has faced sin and defeated it by discipline. Innocence—at least infant innocence—has arrived at sinlessness merely from a lack of maturity. It has not had to face sin and defeat it. It has never much reckoned with sin at all.

In some ways heaven and earth must keep their juxtaposition. The heaven we aim at is no place to build spiritual heroes. That must be done here on earth. That is why author Paul Billheimer wrote: "The character of agape love could not be produced in heaven . . . The conditions required to bring people to spiritual maturity are not found there."[3] Perhaps that is why we don't esteem people for merely going to heaven. After all, Christ bought them that ticket at the cross and gave them easy access with his own hard-won ordeal. What we more admire is how those en route to heaven handle earth—this vale of tears. Watching people die tells us the reality of their creed. If they really believe that when they die he will take them home on high, they live more confidently. If they stand up to death, we respect them. Heaven is a gift to be taken, but we never admire those who merely receive gifts. Our admiration is reserved for those who buy them. And Jesus has purchased our death-confidence for us.

Heaven is a place where sin cannot enter. Only that which is perfect may ever enter there. Perhaps this is in part the reason that Jesus blessed the children with the benediction that it was faith such as theirs of which the kingdom was composed (Matt. 19:14). Innocence makes the journey from earth to heaven short. Sin lengthens the journey and in some cases makes our arrival there impossible.

Those who fail to live a life of adoration not only refuse to prepare themselves for heaven, they at last evolve into selfish creatures who would not enjoy heaven anyway. Those who find no ready love for Christ in this life will not suddenly be transformed merely by dying into Christ-lovers. Our only hope of enjoying heaven when we get there is to have hungered for it in this life.

DEAD RECKONING

So what are these words to mean to us: "If I love Him when I die"? Doesn't everyone plan to love him when he or she dies? Well, certainly most plan to love him when they die, it's just that they don't plan to die very soon.

The schoolmaster in Bronte's *Jane Eyre* calls the title character a very wicked girl and then asks her if she knows where wicked girls go when they die. "To hell, sir," answers Jane Eyre. The schoolmaster reminds her that hell is a place of fire where wicked girls will burn forever. Jane agrees that she is wicked and will likely go to hell when she dies.

"What do you plan to do about it?" asks the schoolmaster.

"I plan to live a very long time, sir," the child answers.

In the novel you are instantly on Jane's side and find yourself wondering what happens to wicked school-masters when they die. But one thing is sure: like Jane Eyre, most of us plan to live a long time. But as the child's hymn suggests, we all plan to "love Him when we die."

Life and death are the categories of metaphor often used to picture those who have trusted Christ and are saved or those who have refused to trust him and are lost. Paul indicated that the way to get over your fear of dying is to "count yourselves dead" (Rom. 6:11). Dead people have no fear of dying. Only the living fear this. People who have given their lives to Christ—really given them—have no reason to fear dying. In his book *Reaching Out,* author Henri Nouwen included this story:

During the Second World War, a Lutheran bishop imprisoned in a German concentration camp was tortured by an S.S. officer who wanted to force him to a confession. In a small room, the two men were facing each other, one afflicting the other with increasing pain. The bishop, who had a remarkable tolerance for pain, did not respond to the torture. His silence, however, enraged the officer to such a degree that he hit his victim harder and harder until he finally exploded and shouted at his victim, "But don't you know that I can kill you?" The bishop looked in the eyes of his torturer and said slowly, "Yes, I know—do what you want—but I have already died . . ." At that moment the S.S. officer could no longer raise his arm and lost power over his victim. It was as if he was paralyzed, no longer able to touch him. All his cruelties had been based on the supposition that this man would hold on to his own life as to his most valuable property, and would be quite willing to give his confession in exchange for his life. But with the grounds for his violence gone, torture had become a ridiculous and futile activity.[4]

Here is the clear example of one who had reckoned himself dead to sin but alive in Christ.

But does this amount to anything more than a "snow job" on our psyche? Is this anything more than living a half-life of otherworldly devotion while we continue to live in this world?

Perhaps it is possible to play dead till we *are* dead. It is a matter of convincing ourselves that we are dead to current secular values and foolish hedonistic pursuits. Reckoning ourselves dead is the apostle's way of certifying our "true life."

A few weeks ago, Princess, our daughter's dog, began to bark in fury at something hanging low in the big tree at the edge of the backyard. When my daughter went to see the source of the dog's attention, she discovered a possum hanging by its tail. The possum seemed entirely dead, with no life in any of its limbs except for the death grip with which its ratlike tail clung to the tree limb.

Princess, in her agitated state, not only barked at the possum but actually struck its inverted head with her paws. Yet the possum never moved. Only when the dog and her mistress were back in the house did the possum leave the tree and yard.

It is homey but not a bad metaphor for Romans 6:11.

The possum had reckoned itself dead, sufficiently enough to convince its predator it was dead. Satan, our predator who pursues us like a lion on the prowl (1 Peter 5:8) can never threaten those of us who play dead to his deceits.

We can play dead as a kind of preparation for that time when we are dead. This is how the saved cope with their sins. There is an odd sense that all sins are dealt with by dying, yet it is Jesus' death that first deals with our sins. But once we are saved, it is our own death that reckons with our sins.

John Bunyan has given us a picture of how he felt once he received the forgiveness of his sins:

> *Thus far did I come laden with my sin;*
> *Nor could aught ease the grief that I was in,*
> *Till I came hither: what a place is this!*
> *Must here be the beginning of my bliss?*
> *Must here the burden fall from off my back?*
> *Must here the strings that bound it to me crack?*
> *Blest cross! Blest sepulcher! Blest rather be*
> *The Man that there was put to shame for me!*[5]

So it was in Christ's dying that we were saved, but it is in *our* dying that we are daily sanctified. We must not just carry our cross but climb upon it of our own accord and reckon ourselves "crucified with Christ" (Gal. 2:20). Then we will have died to our own ambitions, our own values. Heaven will then be our only option, for we will no longer exist to serve any false value.

THE GLEAM OF FINALITY

As for our actual entrance into heaven, we cannot know when that will come. Since we cannot know when it will occur, the implication is plain: we ought to love him every day in case that day turns out to be the one on which we actually die. But we should never love Jesus just because loving him is a good thing to do before death. We ought to love Jesus because Jesus is worthy of our love. We ought to love him because he made us (Ps. 100:3). We ought to love him because he is our very present help in trouble (Ps. 46:1). We ought to love him because He is both the bread of life (John 6:48) and the daily bread of our table (Matt. 6:11). He is the serpent on the pole (John 3:14) and when he is exalted, he draws us toward God (John 12:32). He is the vine through which we find life (John 15:4) and our highway to God (John 14:6). He keeps a crown of coronation ready for us the very moment we step from earth to glory (2 Tim. 4:8). No wonder Augustine said to love all things for God's sake but love God for his own sake.

"If I love Him when I die" is earth's most reasonable hypothesis. Why should we die in any other frame of mind than that of loving God? Yet as important as this "dying love" of God is, most people die pretty much as they have lived. Consider the tale of two men. Both of them were affable and even laughable at times. Certainly they were pleasant in the best seasons of life. They were both passionate in their support of college football.

Within a short period of time I saw both of them die with cancer. One of these men, James, long before his death—even before he knew he had cancer—came into a relationship with Christ. He continued to enjoy football but his passion was spent on God. He loved God and in a reasonably short time had influenced both of his sons into trusting Christ as their Savior.

His love set his face agleam with hope. He prayed for healing from cancer and we all joined him in his prayer. Alas, his sickness progressed till it stole his weight and health. At last even his flesh tones grew ashen and pale. But his eyes, even in his seasons of debilitating pain, kept their sparkle and his confidence in God soared. It seemed to me he never really died, he just rafted the cascades of inner confidence directly into the presence of God. "If I love Him when I die" would never be enough for this good man of faith. He had to love him while he lived, for he found it a lightsome thing to love God.

But consider the second man. He died of cancer, never loving God when he died, for he had never loved him while he lived. He died on a Saturday, which was college football day. I went in to talk to him about his faith in Christ. I actually went to see if I could reason with him about coming to faith in Christ. I was in his hospital room making my "pitch" for God at two o'clock when the time for the game arrived. I saw him feebly sit up in bed and reach for the control knob of the TV set. He said, "Big Red"—the name of the football team he weakly cheered for. Then he turned on the TV and settled back in silence. He had only an odd passion for sports as his final moments came. He died loving not God but only football. So he did die pretty much as he had lived, loving God in death no more than he had ever loved him in life.

If we are to love him when we die, we had best love him while we live.

CONCLUSION

Since we cannot know the moment life will end, and since it is ordered by the Scriptures that we ought to love God when we die, the perfect answer to all our uncertainty is to love Christ while we live. Amos 4:12 teaches us, "Prepare to meet your God." How do we get ourselves ready for this meeting? We love! Widely, openly, freely. But most of all, we love Jesus. We must love him all the days of our life so we can be sure we love him when we die.

"If I love Him when I die," he will, as the song promises, "take me home on high." Did ever winged creatures soar on higher winds than this? So I must love him daily, in case this day should be my last. And should it be I will find myself aloft with eagles. I shall wake a world away, soaring still.

QUESTIONS FOR REFLECTION

1. Have you ever been around a child who was dying? How did he or she handle it? Did you experience a sense of victory in the child's ordeal? Explain in what way you felt it.
2. Do think a Christian would have to be living a very close-to-God life to be able to say what Paul said in Philippians 1:21 ("I am torn between the two: I desire to depart and to be with Christ, which is better by far; but it is more necessary for you that I remain in the body")?
3. What do you think the dying child meant by referring to heaven as "a house with many windows"?
4. What did Paul have in mind when he said we should reckon ourselves dead to sin (Rom. 6:11)?

5. According to this chapter how should obsessor fans balance their love of, say, football, with their love for Christ? For that matter, how do we know when we are giving undue attention to anything in life? How do we achieve a healthy balance between loving God and any other area of our lives?

Jesus Loves Me! This I Know

A child's hymn may well be the dwelling place of angels, the residence of the Savior, the address of God.

I was visiting a small private university some years ago when the chancellor said he had just received a vision of a nine-hundred-foot Christ. The entire nation seemed stirred either to believe or mock the apparition. For most it was a prosaic matter and didn't seem to matter one way or the other.

But I was the guest lecturer on the campus that week, and it did matter to me. I was speaking in chapel on the very day of the vision and felt compelled to make some comment. When I spoke that morning, I affirmed the chancellor for seeing a Christ of three hundred meters (somehow it didn't seem so overlarge in the metric system). Then I invited the students to consider the smaller image of the thumbnail Christ of Teresa of Avila. It is this smaller Savior who rules our microworlds from his address in our hearts. Teresa of Avila was a Carmelite nun and contemporary of Martin Luther. Unlike Luther, she remained a Catholic all her life. But in most ways her devotion focused fully on Christ and her will to let him rule her soul from its center.

How important that Christ indwell our hearts, for we

have no innate godhood of our own. If ever we are to know the indwelling of God, we must beg the Savior to fill our neediness.

"Jesus Loves Me" abandons all notion of the God who merely exists somewhere in favor of the God whom we need now. This is not the God of philosophers and theologians. This is the God of "Now I lay me down to sleep." When Christians speak of what it means to become a Christian they often explain conversion as the act of taking Jesus "into their hearts." It's an emotive, romantic sort of way of referring to faith. Still, bringing Christ into our hearts conjures up a new geography of the soul. Jesus is not "out there," seeking my adoration. Rather, he pursues my devotion from inside me, loving me.

Jesus loves me and through faith I give him his inner residence in my life. This inner Jesus proves that there is not only somebody beyond me who likes me but someone within me who does. Likes? Nay, loves! And the world itself is proof of his love. Nature calls to us in myriad doxologies: the finch's serenade, the awesome declarations of white thunderheads, the roar of seas against stony cliffs. All these say, "God is in love with us and his love matters."

But if I push the issue further than mere nature, I can see a cross on a hill. Then all doubt that Jesus loves me is erased by the sound of hammers ringing out on nails and the labored, final breathing of my executed Lover.

But am I merely being poetic here or am I examining some granite truth? What is it that prods my need to know I am loved? Is this how people arrive at significance, by mixing God into their generous recipes for self-worth? No. "Jesus Loves Me" is the best way to put some point in the pointlessness of existence. We teach our children the song so they can find a reason to go on when the emptiness of their living would otherwise crush them into insignificance. The only antidote to meaningless living is love, and from this vantage point we can see the realm of all that matters.

I once knew of a mother with a child who was incapacitated with a very severe form of cerebral palsy. I always marveled that this mom seemed to thrive in her zest for life, when she had very few friends who ever called on her. Because her son's condition demanded her constant care, she rarely left him alone with others, even to have lunch with a friend.

Yet she rose every morning and dressed in near-elegant fashion. Her appearance was never unkempt but always neat and proper. She spoon-fed and diapered her son until his death as a teenager. He had never learned to say her name. He had never been able to form the phrase, "I love you." Yet it seemed to me she was free of all hang-ups that would have tried to force him to speak words of love she longed to hear but knew he could not frame. Nor did she display any of those idiosyncrasies that come from large doses of psychotic loneliness. Why such wholeness in so debilitating a suffrage? She had someone to love.

We are God's pleasure. His someone to love.

We can see we are loved. How do we know? Jesus best reveals himself and his love to us in the Bible. Here is the Word of God, his letter of love. Listen to it:

Almighty love is
Resonating through the Pentateuch.
Swelling in the histories,
Bursting symphonically
In Psalms and tympani,
Parading through the prophets,

Marching through the gospels
Living in the letters of St. Paul.
Walking the glass sea
Above the final throne of time
In John's grand Revelation.
It is God's letter of love.
And all of it exists to thunder one resounding shout,
"Jesus loves you!"

You are loved. Jesus certifies it all. Where Jesus loves, the world begins. Believe it and live above the ordinary. Teach the sun the glory of its rising. Tutor every star to praise its place in heaven. Bless the snow's pure ermine grace. See the rain as shredded platinum.

Jesus loves you. The Bible tells you so.

QUESTIONS FOR REFLECTION

1. Do you think some people have problems letting God love them? Do you? How do you get past this barrier to a real relationship with God?
2. Make a list of ten ways you know Jesus loves you, then make this your "thank list" for the rest of the week.
3. Can you think of an instance when you found God's Word a personal and healing letter of love?

NOTES

Chapter 1

1. Jean-Baptiste-Henri Lacordaire as quoted in Calvin Miller, *The Book of Jesus* (New York: Simon & Schuster, 1996), 52.

2. G. K. Chesterton as quoted in Brent Curtis and John Eldredge, *The Sacred Romance* (Nashville, TN: Thomas Nelson Publishers, 1997), 35.

3. Mother Teresa as quoted in Tricia McCary Rhodes, *Taking Up Your Cross* (Minneapolis: Bethany House Publishers, 2000), 167.

4. Brent Curtis and John Eldredge, *Sacred Romance*, 15.

5. Donald Hudson as quoted in Curtis and Eldredge, *Sacred Romance*, 204.

6. Gerald May as quoted in Curtis and Eldredge, *Sacred Romance*, 149.

7. Richard Foster, *Celebration of Discipline* (San Francisco: Harper–San Francisco, 1988).

Chapter 2

1. F. B. Meyer, *Our Daily Homily* (London: Marshall, Morgan & Scott, 1951), 183.

2. Henri J. Nouwen as quoted in Rhodes, *Taking Up Your Cross*, 15.

3. Curtis and Eldredge, *Sacred Romance,* 20.

4. Ravi Zacharias, *Jesus Among Other Gods* (Nashville, TN: Word Publishing, 2000), 38.

5. Fanny J. Crosby, "Saved by Grace," 1891.

6. Thomas Brooks as quoted in John Blanchard, *Gathered Gold* (Durham, England: Evangelical Press, 1984), 171–73.

7. Charles H. Spurgeon as quoted in Miller, *Book of Jesus,* 546.

Chapter 3

1. Theodore Roosevelt, April 10, 1899.

2. As quoted in John Blanchard, *Gathered Gold,* 168–69.

Chapter 4

1. Curtis and Eldredge, *Sacred Romance,* 5.

2. Louis Evely, *That Man Is You,* trans. Edmond Bonin (New York: Paulist Press, 1963), 3.

3. Malcolm Muggeridge, *The Green Stick* (New York: William Morrow and Company, Inc., 1972), 82.

4. Mother Teresa in *Mother Teresa: Contemplative in the Heart of the World,* comp. Angelo Devananda (Ann Arbor, MI: Servant Books, 1985), 75.

5. Mother Teresa, "Daily Prayer" in *Eerdman's Book of Famous Prayers,* comp. Veronica Zundel (Grand Rapids, MI: William B. Eerdman Publishing Company, 1983), 99.

6. Norman Kemp Smith as quoted in Timothy George, "Big Picture Faith," *Christianity Today,* 23 October 2000, 91.

7. Ibid.

8. Ibid.

9. Fyodor Dostoyevsky, *The Brothers Karamazov* (New York: Everymans Library, 1992).

10. Philip Yancey, "Getting a Life," *Christianity Today*, 23 October 2000, 128.

Chapter 5

1. Elijah P. Brown as quoted in Miller, *Book of Jesus*, 117.

2. Edwin Arlington Robinson as quoted in Miller, *Book of Jesus*, 459.

3. Amy Carmichael as quoted in Elisabeth Elliot, *Heroes* (Ann Arbor, MI: Servant Publications, 1983), 28.

4. Ibid.

Chapter 6

1. William Griffin as quoted in Miller, *Book of Jesus*, 208.

2. Saint Alphonsus Maria de Liguori as quoted in Miller, *Book of Jesus*, 257.

3. Augustine of Hippo as quoted in Miller, *Book of Jesus*, 228–29.

Chapter 7

1. Richard Blanchard, "Worship His Majesty." Copyright 1964 by Sacred Songs, a division of Word, Inc.

2. Ted Bundy in *Focus on the Family Magazine*, March 1989, 23.

3. Angela Morgan, adapted from Alec Davidson.

4. Karl Menninger, *Whatever Became of Sin* (New York: Hawthorn Books, 1973), 105–6, quoting from "Claude Eatherly—War Hero," review of Robert Jungk's *The Unending Nightmare of Claude Eatherly, Hiroshima Pilot* in *Liberation*, 6:19 (January, 1962).

5. Donna Swanson as quoted in Miller, *Book of Jesus*, 242–43.

6. Charles H. Spurgeon as quoted in Miller, *Book of Jesus*, 558.

7. Hudson Taylor as quoted in Miller, *Book of Jesus*, 587.

8. Brother Lawrence, *The Practice of the Presence of God* (Philadelphia: The Judson Press, n.d.), 26.

Chapter 8

1. William Jennings Bryan, *The Prince of Peace* (Chicago: Reilly and Briton Co., 1909), 20–27.

2. David Shapiro and Richard Leider as quoted in Laurie Beth Jones, *The Path* (New York: Hyperion, 1996), x.

3. Isaac Watts, "At the Cross," 1707.

4. Jones, *The Path*, 67.

5. Don Herold as quoted in Wayne Cordeiro, *Developing an Attitude That Attracts Success* (Honolulu: New Hope Resources, 1999), 27.

6. Mother Teresa as quoted in Wayne Cordeiro, *Doing Church as a Team* (Honolulu: New Hope Publishers, 1998), 98.

7. Ibid., 82.

8. Robert Frost, "Two Tramps in Mud Time,"

9. Dag Hammarskjöld as quoted in James William McClenden, *Biography as Theology* (San Francisco: Perkley Press, 1974), 113.

10. Cordiero, *Doing Church as a Team,* 33-34.

11. Edmond John Carnell as quoted in George, "Big Picture Faith," 93.

Chapter 9

1. David Livingston, *Anthology of Jesus* (Kregel Publications, 1981).

2. Johnny Hart, *B.C.,* syndicated, 19 August 1990.

3. Jean Pierre De Caussade, *The Sacrament of the Present Moment,* trans. Kitty Muggeridge (Cambridge: Harper and Row, 1982).

4. Madeleine L'Engle, *Weather of the Heart* (Chicago: Shaw Press, 1969), 38.

5. De Caussade, *The Sacrament of the Present Moment.*

6. T. H. White, *The Book of Merlyn* (Ace Books, 1999), 45–48.

Chapter 10

1. C. Austin Miles. Copyright 1912 by Hall-Mack Co. Renewed 1940 by the Rodeheaver Co., a division of Word, Inc.

2. Robert Coles, "The Inexplicable Prayers of Ruby Bridges," *Christianity Today,* 9 August 1985, 17–18.

3. Ibid.

4. Thomas à Kempis, *The Imitation of Christ* (New York: Doubleday, Image Books, 1955), 103.

5. Laura A. Barter Snow as quoted in Paul E. Billheimer, *Don't Waste Your Sorrows* (Ft. Washington, PA: Christian Literature Crusade, 1977), 65–66.

Chapter 11

1. Judith Deem Dupree, *Going Home* (Palm Springs, CA: Ronald N. Haynes Publishers, 1984), 74.

2. Malcolm Muggeridge, *The End of Christendom* (Grand Rapids, MI: William. B. Eerdmans Publishing Co., 1980), 36.

3. Billheimer, *Don't Waste Your Sorrows*, 85.

4. Henri J. M. Nouwen, *Reaching Out* (New York: Doubleday & Co. Inc., 1966), 84.

5. John Bunyan, *Pilgrim's Progress*, ed. N. H. Keeble (New York: Oxford University Press, 1998).